Praise for the work of Brook Noel

"I have read Brook's book. I keep it by my bed side and still pick it up when I remember something that was said but don't remember how it was said. I have read many grief support books and have found this to be the best by far." ~ Karen

"I am blessed to have you in my life as well the support group."~ Maureen

"Thanks so much for your wise words. [Your work] is really helping me cope." ~ Stephanie

"I just wanted to tell you that I love the book *I Wasn't Ready to Say Goodbye.* My boyfriend of ten years just passed away the day after Easter. Well I was looking around on the internet and I came across your book. I read some of the comments from readers that have read your book and it moved me to go down to my local bookstore to pick it up. I love it! I understood the feelings of going crazy. And I feel like the book you and Pamela wrote will help me to deal with him passing on. I just wanted to say thanks and keep up the good work." ~Michelle

"I generally don't write e-mails but I had to write to you. I am a 52 year old widow, my husband died of cancer seven years ago leaving me with two wonderful daughters. Yesterday I bought and read yo

Now I am going to have my oldest daughter who is 21 read it. I think it will help her too. Thank you for letting me know I am sane, and I am feeling all the things I need and am going to feel. I too have started to write a book... and maybe if I finish it, it will help someone as you helped me. Thank you again." ~ Ona

"Dear Brook and Pam: I am a bereaved parent who just finished reading *I Wasn't Ready to Say Goodbye,* and I can't thank you enough for the inspiration and knowledge that I got from your pages."~ Christine

"Written from knowledge and from a place of understanding and guidance is sure to make this book a winner and a timeless treasure for anyone who has known a deep loss." ~Bernadette Moyer Sahm

"I purchased this book shortly after my 31 year old brother, Chad, became the victim of a homicide. What a relief to read that I was not alone in my feelings, that I wasn't going crazy! This book helped me deal with emotions that I had never dealt with before and get me through some rough times!" ~ Julie

"I lost my Mom 3 months ago. This book has helped me through my grief. It explains all the stages of grief. I felt like I could really relate to everything, which helped because the people around me are not grieving, and don't feel what I am feeling." ~ Heather

Grief Steps®

10 Steps to Regroup, Rebuild and Renew After Any Life Loss

by Brook Noel

CHAMPION PRESS, LTD.

CHAMPION PRESS, LTD.
FREDONIA, WISCONSIN

ISBN: 1891400355
LCCN: 2002103085

Manufactured in the United States of America 20 19 18 17 16 15 14 13 12 11

Dedication

If grief has taught me one thing, it is that life is a cycle of "comings" and "goings," and that we can learn valuable lessons from both processes. I would like to dedicate this book to those who are currently in my life that I have learned so much from, and care for so deeply...

Wendy	Sara	Craig
Mike	Andy	Sammy
Shelly	Carrie	Char
Chuck	Kim	GS Online Friends

And likewise, for the people I have lost through the ebbs and flows of life. Thank you for your lessons. I will remember you always...

Caleb	Becky	Brian
Jennifer	Gina	Greg
Jack	Joan	Jim
Luis	Art	Scott
Forest	Paco	Samson

Also by Brook Noel and Pamela D. Blair, Ph.D.

I Wasn't Ready to Say Goodbye: surviving, coping and healing after the sudden death of a loved one

I Wasn't Ready to Say Goodbye Companion Workbook

Living with Grief: a guide to your first year of grieving

You're Not Alone: Resources to Help You through Your Journey

My World Is Upside Down: Making Sense of Life After Confronting A Death

Also by Brook Noel

Back to Basics: 101 Ideas for Strengthening Our Children and Our Families

The Single Parent Resource

Understanding the Emotional and Physical Effects of Grief

Finding Peace: Exercises to Help Heal the Pain of Loss

Grief Steps: 10 Steps to Rebuild, Rebuild and Renew After Any Loss Companion Workbook

Surviving Holidays, Birthdays and Anniversaries: a guide to grieving during special occasions

Available at www.championpress.com

Visit Brook Noel's support site at www.griefsteps.com

Acknowledgments

Every book is a culmination of energies that allows a book to "be." Grief Steps is no different. In fact, perhaps with its emotional topics and involvement, it relied on the help of others even moreso.

First, my thanks to MaryAnn Koopmann, who continually pointed me in the right direction, and reminded me of my goals on the days I had a hard time "figuring out what it was all for."

Extreme thanks and appreciation go out to all the wonderful people who have joined the on-line Grief Steps Support Group. The faith and trust you have shown in sharing your stories makes you all "emotional heroes" (as Wendy would say). Your appreciation and kindness make the world a better place. A special thanks to my co-moderators... Anne, Maureen and Heather.

I also want to thank the many readers who have read my work and taken the time to write. Each of your letters has touched my heart. And I also thank the many readers who have read my work, but have not written. It is an investment of resources, and more importantly, an investment of time to undertake reading a book. I am pleased that you have valued my work and made room for it in your life.

"Sorrows are our best
educators.
[One] can see further
through a tear
than a telescope."

~ Lord Byron

Contents

An Introduction to Grief Steps®

"What we call the beginning
is often the end.
       To make an end is to
make a beginning.
       The end is where
              we start from."

~ T.S. Eliot

There are moments in life where time seems to stand still. Moments where life as we knew it, and life as it will be, collide in tragedy or loss. A valuable relationship may end. We may lose someone we love. We might be fired. An illness or accident may take away functionality that we aren't prepared to lose. A family pet may die. A child may run away, move out or be kidnapped. We might choose or be forced to relinquish an addiction we can't imagine living without. We might be wrapped in depression and unable to "snap out of it." Whatever the trauma, we face that moment of loss with a hurting heart, ill-equipped to handle the impending life change.

Whether our loss is anticipated or sudden, the moment where loss becomes reality leaves our breath caught in our throat, our blood cold, and all we can murmur is… "Why?" Tomorrow loses importance in the face of today's grief, as we wonder how to go on.

These questions have plagued me intensely over the past decade. They plagued me when my perfectly healthy, only sibling, was stung by a bee and died within the hour, at age 27. They plagued me when my husband's company gave us three weeks to move cross-country to a region I had hoped to leave behind forever. They plagued me when my parents divorced and my estranged father continually fell short, offering only false promises. They plagued me when a dear friend was killed in a drunk-driving accident, another lost to leukemia, and yet another to brain cancer. And, as they plague me, they plague so many others. They plague the many "9/11" survivors I have spoken to and worked with. They plague men and women who have watched their marriages and relationships fail. They plague the parents of children who are diagnosed with unexpected illness. They plague the hearts of pet owners who lose their fury companions. They even plague the person who seems to "have it all," yet feels so empty within. Undeniably, loss becomes just as much a part of life as gain.

At some point we all experience the pain of loss and we each react differently. What one person might consider significant trauma may have little impact on another person. But at some point we will all come face to face with the type of loss that leaves us fumbling and breathless.

The first book I co-authored with Pamela D. Blair on loss, *I Wasn't Ready to Say Goodbye: surviving, coping and healing after the sudden death of a loved one,* is a book I wish I'd never had to author. It was written after the sudden death of my brother. Being a writer, I turned to books for help and was amazed to find that, at the time, there weren't any books dealing specifically with unexpected death. In my brother's honor, I set out to create the most complete book on the topic. With the help of my co-author, I feel we achieved that goal.

That book opened the door to a world I had never expected to enter. It was a world with stories of pain, loss and bittersweet memories. While I had once thought it rare to feel such intense grief, I quickly learned that the world was full of aching hearts behind closed doors. This world contained millions of grievers, who often walked alone, looking for a hand to hold to make it through to another day.

I have learned many valuable lessons in this world of grief. I have also noticed something. After the loss, after the grief work, after the pain, some people readjust and actually live a fuller life. They regroup, re-prioritize, and reconcile themselves to their loss and to their world. They use their pain as a springboard to reach higher ground.

Others do not. Other grievers seem buried beneath their grief, in a constant struggle to find the air to keep them going. The world becomes a dark place with little room for them. Their health declines, and worst of all, their hope declines.

And so the question of "why" surfaced again. This time, I wondered why some people were able to heal and create a springboard from their grief while others wrapped themselves so tightly in their pain they became immobilized.

This phenomenon wasn't just among those who survived the loss of a loved one. The same patterns occurred with those who had lost a valuable relationship, a much-loved pet, a job, a home, a part of themselves.

I set out to answer the following question: What had happened in the lives of those who coped successfully that wasn't happening in the lives of those who couldn't bounce back—even after years had passed? After three years, I began to discover what I now call "Grief Steps®"—actions we must take in order to successfully climb out of the depths of our grief. Although how we each react to our grief is unique, it became apparent that the Steps to escape that darkness are universal. What's more, Grief Steps® can work for any level of loss—whether it be a minor setback or a full-scale catastrophe.

In this book, I aim to share these Grief Steps® with you. They are not rigid concepts, but more of a flowing process. Instead of being ten tidy cups of water, they are like a river, flowing back and forth, slowly then faster, until they lead us to the mouth of the river where life awaits us once again.

While each loss carries unique challenges, this book focuses on the universal characteristics of grief. To explore every type of loss would make this book 1000+ pages and leave little of the text relevant to your specific situation. For that reason, I focus on the fundamental, universal Steps we must all take to move successfully through grief.

Despite its pitfalls and potholes, life is a glorious journey. Life is a gift and we are the recipients. As long as it is in our hands, it deserves to be lived. And you deserve the sweetness that comes from living your life fully. May these Steps help you find your way toward that life.

The 10 Grief Steps®

This book is organized by order into 10 Grief Steps®. You'll find a chapter devoted to each Step. Here is a summary of the Steps we will take on our journey.

Step One: Shock and Survival
Purpose: To survive the shock of our loss while tending to the basics of reality

.

Step Two: The Emotional Rollercoaster
Purpose: To decompress from our shock; and to identify and understand the full range of emotions that accompany our loss.

Step Three: Acknowledgment and Active Grieving
Purpose: To acknowledge the reality of our loss and then acquire the tools and exercises to grieve in a healthy way.

Step Four: Understanding Our Story
Purpose: To find a beginning, middle and end so that we may cease obsessive thinking.

Step Five: Finding Forgiveness
Purpose: To release ourselves from unnecessary pain through the act of forgiveness.

Step Six: Finding Faith
Purpose: To explore, rebuild and repair our faith.

Step Seven: Finding Meaning
Purpose: To understand that even the deepest tragedy can bring meaning, and to uncover that meaning.

Step Eight: Redefining Ourselves
Purpose: To understand the void that has been created by our loss and how that void will change our personal belief system.

Step Nine: Living With Our Loss
Purpose: To integrate our newly discovered meaning into our day-to-day lives and to move forward despite our loss.

Step Ten: Accepting Our New Life
Purpose: To take responsibility that life is ours to be lived to its fullest.

How to Use the Grief Steps® to Get the Most Out of This Book

"We go through the motions
until they become real again."

~ John Steinbeck

This book is as much about action as it is about healing. There isn't a way to get around the pain that comes with loss. In order to move past it, we must move through it. For that reason, you will be asked to contemplate, ruminate and discover many things about yourself, your loss, and the world we live in. I have created a *Grief Steps® Companion Workbook* (available at www.griefsteps.com) to accompany this book. It provides spaces for many of the exercises in this book and additional exercises as well. I strongly encourage you to pick up a copy and use it as you read through this book. You may want to read through this book once and then go back and read it a second time, while completing the workbook-exercises. At a minimum, have a blank journal handy to record your thoughts, emotions and answers to the questions within these pages.

Throughout each chapter you will find HOPE NOTES. These HOPE NOTES highlight the major lessons, wisdom and healing activities that we need to carry forward and practice from each Grief Step®.

I also recommend joining the free Grief Steps® support site at www.griefsteps.com. When you join you will receive a Welcome Packet that explains how to use the different areas of the service. Membership includes a 24/7 support message board, twice-monthly chats and a free support newsletter. We also anticipate online support meetings structured specifically around this book. You can learn more about these meetings and other Grief Step® services at the website.

Where Do I Start In My Grief Work?

Much of your grief work will depend on how intricately your loss is woven into your life fabric. Some losses affect only specific areas of our life while leaving other areas unaffected. Other losses seem to touch every part of our being.

When a loss is not completely permeating, it doesn't mean it isn't significant. It simply means that it may require a different series of Grief Steps®. Some of the Steps will be more relevant to your situation, while others will require less time to work through.

When a loss does permeate every fiber of our being, all of the Grief Steps® become necessary for full healing. It is important to pay special attention to the Steps that you want to "skim by" or "ignore." These Steps are often where you need to do the most work.

No matter when your loss occurred, the Grief Steps® can work for you. You may be grieving something that happened days ago or years ago, no matter—unresolved grief does not age. It sits in our souls until we deal with it and work through it. Old wounds and new can be healed through Grief Step work.

I have included a questionnaire on the following pages. You may use it to help you decide which Grief Steps® are most important for your journey. While I recommend reading through the whole book, you don't need to do it in order. This questionnaire is designed to direct you toward the concepts you need to work with the most, or address first.

> **Hope Note:** *It is important to pay special attention to Steps that you want to "skim by" or "ignore." These Steps are often where you need to do the most work.*

Exploring Grief

This is not a quiz but a questionnaire to help you analyze where to begin your grief work. Grief is not an exact science, so creating a quiz to evaluate where you are in the process would prove extremely challenging. However, the questions on these pages allow you to assess what parts of the grieving process you have completed successfully. Following the questions, you will also find a summary of what your answers mean. Your answers will guide you toward the Steps that will be most helpful to you at this time. Most readers will have two or more Steps they need to work with. When that is the case, begin with the lowest numbered Step and work toward the higher numbered Step. For example, if you found that you scored highest in "Step Five: Finding Forgiveness" and then next in "Step Ten: Accepting Life," begin your grief work with Step Five and then complete Step Ten.

1. My loss occurred within   ____ Y ____ N
   the last 3 months.

2. I feel numb, like I can't believe   ____ Y ____ N
   this happened.

3. Sometimes I feel like everything   ____ Y ____ N
   is happening in slow motion.

4. If someone asked "How do you   ____ Y ____ N
   feel?" I could identify my emotions.

5. I have felt intense sadness.   ____ Y ____ N

6. I have felt intense anger.   ____ Y ____ N

7. I understand what happened   ____ Y ____ N
   and why.

8. My mind is clear and I have quit   ____ Y ____ N
   thinking about this situation constantly.

9. I have given myself time and space   ____ Y ____ N
   to grieve as needed.

10. If the loss occurred over several   ____ Y ____ N
    months ago, I have continued to cry occasionally since
    that time.

11. I talk openly about my loss.   ____ Y ____ N

12. Despite my sadness, I have been   ____ Y ____ N
    able to see the reason why this may have happened.

13. I have reached out to others   ____ Y ____ N
    in a similar situation and offered my help.

14. I understand what has happened and do not think
    about my loss constantly.   ____ Y ____ N

15. I have identified the void left by my loss and have
    begun to take action to fill it.   ____ Y ____ N

16. I have continued communicating, in a healthy way,
    with my friends.   ____ Y ____ N

17. I have maintained (or returned to) the hobbies I
    was engaged in before my loss.   ____ Y ____ N

18. I feel bitter inside.   ____ Y ____ N

19. I feel angry inside.   ____ Y ____ N

If you have a religious background, please answer questions
20-23. If not, please go to question 24.

20. I have quit going to church.   ____ Y ____ N

21. I have quit praying. _____ Y _____ N

22. I question how God could let this happen.

_____ Y _____ N

23. I don't feel my faith community understands what I am going through. _____ Y _____ N

24. I have created rituals to honor my loss.

_____ Y _____ N

25. I can think about my loss without extreme sadness. _____ Y _____ N

26. I am engaging in new hobbies and trying new things. _____ Y _____ N

27. I have made new friends. _____ Y _____ N

28. I have returned to work. _____ Y _____ N

29. I feel hope more often than I feel hopelessness.

_____ Y _____ N

30. I see a purpose for my life. _____ Y _____ N

Hope Note: *Grief is never easy... but we need to be easy on ourselves.*

Evaluating Your Answers

Questions 1-3

If you answered "yes" to any of these questions, you are likely still experiencing some level of shock. Begin with Step One: Shock and Survival.

Questions 4-6

If you answered "no" to any of these questions, you may not be facing your feelings fully. Work with Step Two: The Emotional Rollercoaster.

Questions 7-8

If you answered "no" to either of these questions, you likely do not understand the story of your loss. Work with Step Four: Understanding Your Story.

Questions 9-11

If you answered "no" to any of these questions, you have probably not grieved as actively as needed or acknowledged your loss completely. Work with Step Three: Acknowledgement and Active Grieving.

Questions 12-13

If you answered "no" to either of these questions, you still need to uncover some meaning behind your loss. Work with Step Seven: Finding Meaning.

Questions 14-17

If you answered "no" to two or more of these questions, you may not have completed the process of redefining yourself and your world. Work with Step Eight: Redefining Ourselves.

Questions 18-19

If you answered "yes" to either of these questions, you may have unresolved forgiveness issues. Work with Step Five: Finding Forgiveness.

Questions 20-23

If you answered "yes" to two or more of these questions, you likely need more support through your faith. Work with Step Six: Finding Faith.

Questions 24-25

If you answered "no" to either of these questions, it is unlikely that you have incorporated your loss into daily living. Please work with Step Nine: Living With Our Loss.

Questions 26-30

If you answered "no" to any of these questions, it is unlikely you have fully accepted life after your loss. Please work with Step Ten: Accepting Your New Life.

Basic Guidelines for Grief Work

Before we begin our journey, I want to outline some basic concepts for our grief work. These are simple reminders for your reference throughout the Grief Steps® process. Read through these periodically, perhaps at the completion of each Step. The statements and the Self-Checks that follow will remind you to be patient and soft with yourself. Grief is never easy, but we need to be easy on ourselves.

I will be patient with myself and understand that grief often involves moving one step forward and two steps back.

I will reach out to others for help when I need support.

I will avoid abusing substances as a way to temporarily minimize my pain.

I will care for myself physically.

I will not isolate myself from friends, hobbies and activities.

I will avoid making major life decisions until I have worked through the Grief Steps®.

I will grieve in my own time and not by how others think I should grieve.

I will create the space and time to honor my emotions.

I will understand that grief recovery takes time, and commit to the Steps—even if relief occurs slower than I would like.

I will remember that moving through grief often involves feeling painful and intense emotions.

I will remember that when I complete my grief work successfully, I can have a rich, although different, life.

Depression and Anxiety

As you work through your grief, it is important to monitor yourself and the stages you are going through. It's important to remember that the psychiatric profession has advanced by leaps and bounds over the past decades. Many doctors are very adept at dealing with emotional and cognitive disorders—from anxiety to depression. Many people have sought professional help with successful results.

> **Hope Note:** *If you think you might benefit from professional help or medication, at least make an appointment for assessment and learn about your options. Doing so is not a sign of weakness, but a sign of strength. It shows that you are strong enough to deal with your problems—versus brushing them beneath the surface.*

One piece of advice: make sure you feel comfortable with the professional you choose to work with. You should be able to ask questions without feeling rushed. You should feel your questions are answered completely and thoroughly. You should feel that your provider has a genuine interest in what you are saying and is helping you to comprehend and process your grief. If you are the least bit uncomfortable after one or two visits, request a different professional (if others are available at the practice) or call a different service. These are very personal issues that you are dealing with. It is imperative that you feel comfortable, safe and heard. It is not uncommon to go through several providers before you find someone you "connect" with.

> **Hope Note:** *I will remember that when I complete my grief work successfully, I can have a rich, although different, life.*

Healthy Grieving vs. Unhealthy Grieving

In the table on page 38, I have listed examples of healthy and unhealthy grieving. As you work through the Grief Steps®, refer to this chart periodically. Note which statements describe you. If you repeatedly find yourself grieving in unhealthy ways, seek the help of a support group or professional for guidance in your grief work.

Healthy Grieving	Unhealthy Grieving
Although saddened, you communicate honestly with friends and family.	You are avoiding friends and family for a prolonged period of time (over three weeks).
You tend to your basic self-care needs.	You are not eating well, sleeping well or tending to your basic self-care needs.
You have accepted the reality of your loss.	You are in denial about your loss or still trying to "go back in time" and change the outcome.
Although you may occasionally have a self-destructive thought, it passes quickly and the majority of your focus is on moving forward.	You have persistent, obsessive or strong self-destructive thoughts. (Seek help immediately.)
You have discovered healthy outlets for your anger.	You take your anger out on yourself or those people close to you. (Seek help immediately.)
You realize that your world has changed and are sad about this change, but believe the future may have good things in store for you.	You have become immobilized by depression and cannot see hope for the future. (Seek help immediately.)
You are facing your feelings.	You are masking your feelings through self-medication.
Although intensely sad, you believe that "this too shall pass."	You feel that your pain will never end.

Step One:
Shock and Survival

Purpose: To survive the shock of
our loss, while tending to the
basics of reality.

"And people cooked for me.
And people answered the
phone for me. People cared
for me when I didn't care."

~ **Wendy Feiereisen**

During shock our bodies and minds shut down, relying on the simplest functioning possible. The When faced with grief, When faced with grief, our bodies and minds tend to shut down. The reason is quite simple. Since we are almost always ill-prepared to handle loss, our body seeks to protect us by shutting down the senses. This allows the body to "tune out" the pain. This "tuning out" accounts for many of the ways grievers describe this stage...

I felt like I was in a movie.
The world seemed dreamlike.
Everything seemed to move in slow motion.
I felt complete numbness.
I felt catatonic.
I went crazy—like an animal.

All of these statements and emotions are normal. They all express different ways of the body filtering information—letting just select facts into our consciousness.

When we understand the first emotions that have filtered through, our bodies let more emotion through. The process continues until we can fully comprehend and prepare to face our loss.

This is the "acute" stage of shock. Like you will see in many other areas of grief, there is no exact timetable or schedule. We all grieve in our own way and in our own time.

The intensity of our loss often influences our level of shock. If we are facing a loss where we had time to prepare, the shock phase may be shorter. When the loss is very sudden, it tends to take longer to loosen shock's grip. The shock phase can last anywhere from several days to a couple of months. If you find yourself still in "acute" shock (acute shock can be defined by an inability to accept reality or function in reality) after six weeks, it is a sign that professional help is likely needed. After six weeks, you should be able to see clear signs of progress. You are probably far from "okay" but you have:

1. Identified and begun to understand what has happened.
2. Accepted the loss as reality.
3. Started grieving for the loss in a healthy way. (See the healthy grieving chart on page 38 for an outline of healthy grieving.)

A Note About Substance Abuse

It is important to note the temptation to abuse substances to null the pain of grief. While they can offer a temporary escape, they will not move you past the pain. Instead, they act like a "pause" button. Substances seem to stop grief in its tracks, but don't be fooled, grief waits for you.

Also at this stage, we are extremely vulnerable. It is easy to fall into an addiction, especially when it seems to make our pain easier to withstand. But we aren't solving anything. We are simply delaying our pain. We are also compounding it, since at some point we will have to deal with our addiction—and our grief will be waiting for us too.

If you sense yourself getting caught up in a vice to deal with your sadness, seek professional help or a support group.

> **Hope Note:** *Be cautious about the use of medication or substances to help you through grief. Remember that there is no way to move around grief, we must move through it. Self-medication only delays that process.*

What To Expect: Physical and Emotional Changes

Fear and anxiety increase when we face the unknown. When we understand that we are traveling a path others have traveled and survived, our fear and anxiety often lessen. Below, I have listed common physical and emotional affects encountered within the grief journey. You may experience some or all of these affects. When you feel them, realize they are normal. You are not going crazy. You are not alone. This is part of the process. Instead of worrying or obsessing about these "side affects" focus your energy on the "Three Goals for the First Few Weeks" (that are covered in the following pages):

Chest pain   Restlessness
Sleep difficulties   Dry mouth

Crying	Exhaustion
Weakness	Dizziness
Numbness	Shakiness
Disorientation	Listlessness
Migraines or headaches	Upset stomach
Heart palpitations	Anxiety
Poor appetite (or overeating)	Social avoidance
Shortness of breath	Aches and Pains

Three Goals
For The First Few Weeks

As we move through Step One, I want to encourage you to focus on three goals:

1. Absorb shock and identify your emotions
2. Seek support in daily living
3. Express your feelings and emotions

GOAL ONE:

Absorbing Shock and Identifying Our Emotions

We need to give ourselves time and space for reality to soak in. We need a place where we feel safe to express our emotions. When we need to cry, yell, rant or rave, we need to honor those feelings and have the space to do so. Often, we don't take the time to *truly feel* our emotions. We get so caught up in society's stereotyping—"Just move on," "It's not safe/ masculine to reveal your emotions, "You're making too much out of this,"—that we repress our feelings. They become buried in our souls and stay there until we go back, dig them up, and work through them (a process we discuss in detail in Step Three).

To complicate matters, we cannot put life on hold while we deal with the acute pain of our loss. No matter what we have gone through there are still bills to be paid, children to raise, household duties and obligations. Somehow we have to continue the motions of living.

Later in this book, we cover "Grief Sessions", which are basically "scheduled" times to experience emotions. It can be helpful to set up Grief Sessions for yourself in these first few weeks. Find a place where you feel safe to let go. Then visit that place twenty minutes each day to get in touch with, and experience, your feelings.

Keep in mind that Goal One doesn't involve trying to change your emotions or work through them. Goal One is simply concerned with *feeling* your emotions—whatever they may be.

Hope Note: Find a place where you feel safe to release your feelings and emotions. Try to do this for 20 minutes each day.

GOAL TWO: Seek Support for Daily Living
Continuing through the motions of living brings us to the second goal—support. Make a list of the commitments you

must keep. (If you are in a severe state of disorganization, have a close friend help you with your list, or see the checklist provided in the *Grief Steps® Companion Workbook*.)

> *"It's an odd thing, but when we become immersed in our hard times, we have a tendency to withdraw. Ironically this is precisely the time we should be communicating with each other!*
>
> *I have always been strong (or so I thought) and sometimes I feel I should bear all the pain by myself and not bother anyone else. For one of the first times in my life, after my son's death, I learned to reach out...and that reaching out was not a sign of weakness, but of strength. I could not have 'made it' on my own. Now, hopefully, I am strong enough to help others get beyond the point of where I have been." ~From a Grief Steps Member*

Make a list of people who would be willing to help you keep your commitments. These may be friends who have already offered assistance or those in your community you feel comfortable asking for help. Try to delegate as many of the "daily living" tasks as possible during the first few weeks of acute grief. This will give you more time and energy, for honoring your emotions and healing.

Hope Note: Reaching out isn't easy, but it is necessary.

GOAL THREE: Express Your Emotions

In Goal One we work toward *feeling* our emotions. We give them space to take on a life of their own instead of suppressing them. Goal Three involves taking the emotions we feel and finding a way to express them outwardly as a step toward healing. Although they sound similar, both of these steps are very different and both are needed for healing.

The first goal requires us to get in touch with what we feel and to let it flow through us. In Goal Three, we actively search to understand these emotions, and to make sure we are handling them in a healthy way. For example, you can know that you are angry but choose not to do anything about it. Goal Three requires that we identify our emotions and then actively make a healthy choice about them. We don't let our emotions fester internally causing unneeded physical and emotional turmoil. Instead, we choose to acknowledge the variety of emotions we are feeling and handle them healthily.

Hope Note: Focus on the three goals as you move through Step One.... Absorbing Shock and Honoring Your Feelings, Finding Support for Daily Living and Expressing Your Emotions in a healthy way.

What If
I'm Past The Acute Grief Stage?

If you are coming to this book several months or years after your loss, you may well be beyond the focus of Step One. You might read Step One and think—"I didn't do those things—what now?" Don't worry. While you may not have accepted and felt your emotions as thoroughly as you would have had you completed these exercises, there are still plenty of ways to dig up the past so that you can face it successfully and move forward with your grief work. No matter when we experience our grief, if we have not dealt with it, it remains in wait. There will be exercises to help you recall past unresolved grief in Step Three.

Even before exploring Step Three, I do recommend that you begin keeping a journal. This journal will become a very valuable tool as you work through your Steps. I recommend journaling at least two pages each night before going to bed. Write down whatever comes to mind. If you are having problems getting started, see the ideas and starters in the *Grief Steps® Companion Workbook* or simply begin with the words… "I feel…" Each time you get stuck, go back and begin again with, "I feel…" It doesn't matter if the writing is grammatically correct or poetic—all that matters is that you are honoring your emotions by expressing them outwardly. Through doing this, we take emotions that we may have hidden or suppressed and move them outside of ourselves where we can deal with them effectively.

If you are not a writer, try keeping a "Voice Journal"

by speaking into a tape recorder. It doesn't matter what method we use, but what is important is to release the emotions through voice or writing. We want to take these emotions from being internal thoughts and give them a physical form. Once we have identified and put our emotions into a physical form, we will be better able to understand our feelings and work through them.

Hope Note: *Choose some form of journaling, whether written or voice, and begin using it daily to release emotions.*

Step One often feels like a slippery ice rink where we are without skates. We are barraged with emotions and challenges at a time when our emotional and physical energy is at a premium. It is important to be easy with yourself, and reduce stress and expectations as much as possible during this period. Taking the time to identify and experience your emotions to their fullest will help immensely as you move forward down grief's pathway.

Step Two:
The Emotional
Rollercoaster

Purpose: To decompress from our shock and to identify and understand the full range of emotions that accompany our loss.

"Problems do not go away. They must be worked through or else they remain, forever a barrier to the growth and development of the spirit."

~ M. Scott Peck

The second Grief Step® involves identifying, understanding and facing our emotions. In order to move through our grief, we must face it.

Often at the time of loss, we are simply incapable of comprehending or coping with our emotions. Then, as life beckons, we push our feelings aside or bury them within. Days, months and sometimes years drift by. We feel a gnawing sadness, but aren't sure of its source—or what to do about it. We know it is dark and ugly so we try to avoid it—often staying as far away from our emotions as possible. Some of us are scared that if we dig into that darkness, we might never come out.

We should be just as afraid of what happens when we don't dig into that darkness. When we leave it there to fester, it becomes the budding ground for our future. Everything we experience must pass through that pile before blossoming.

The process is somewhat like a root canal. We don't want to experience the pain of the root canal, but we don't want to experience the continuing pain of the toothache, either. The only way to obtain lasting comfort is by undergoing the pain of the root canal. To get past the pain, we must move through it. There simply isn't any other way.

For some, this process moves relatively quickly. It's as if a dam has burst and long-suppressed emotions flood forth. For others, the process may require a chisel, to chip away at the wall built within.

As you explore your emotions you may find the help of a support group or a professional extremely valuable. Or you may choose a close friend, pastor, or online support site such as www.griefsteps.com, to share your excavating process. And by all means, if at any point you fear you might inflict harm on yourself or others, seek professional help immediately.

I have always had a difficult time expressing my emotions. I can write about other peoples' feelings and express emotions on paper—but when it comes to verbalizing my own feelings, I often can't find the words. I remember one particular therapist's frustration peaking when he asked me for the fifth time, "How do you feel?" My response was the same as my first four, "I don't know!"

What I learned is that "I don't know" often equals "I don't want to know." We may not want to know what we feel because it scares us. We may not want to know how we feel because then we are responsible for doing something about it.

I am an upbeat and optimistic person. I didn't want to feel the sadness of loss. I felt it would reduce my productivity and affect how I cared for my family. I didn't want people to see me sad. I didn't want anyone to see me weak. But when it comes to grief, ignorance is never bliss. There cannot be bliss again until we have dug out of the darkness.

Later, we will look at some specific tools to use when facing your emotions. For now, let's look at the different emotions that often travel with grief.

Hope Note: When we answer the question, "How do I feel?" with "I don't know," it may mean "I don't want to know." Owning our emotions requires us to take responsibility for them. This responsibility is the only way to move forward in our healing.

The Emotions of Grief

Anger – Anger can be directed at others, yourself, society in general, the world, religion or any other source that you hold responsible for your loss. Anger often stems from blame. When we feel things could be different had "X" not happened, we feel anger toward "X". When we can't find someone or something to hold accountable for our pain, anger may point itself toward our faith or the world at large. Sometimes, it turns inward, becoming self-destructive.

Let's examine the types of anger that are natural, though unhealthy. This wisdom is based on the work of psychotherapist Pamela D. Blair, PhD co-author of *I Wasn't Ready to Say Goodbye.*

Some of us will express anger when we are not getting the support we need from friends, family or work. While intensely wrapped in our grief, we usually don't think to ask for support. Instead we lash out at those close to us with hostility, irritability and anger. If we can recognize this anger for what it is, we can use it in a healthy way. This can be our cue that we need to strengthen our support networks. In some instances, people may be offering support but we are not in an accepting mode. In those times we need to look within. Still at other times, people may be offering support but it might not be the type of support we need. No one is a mind-reader. If our support-needs are going unmet we need to communicate our needs to those trying to help.

Displaced anger is simply misdirected anger. We want someone to take responsibility for what has happened. We need someone to blame and to be held accountable. We may scream or yell at those we feel could have influenced the outcome of this life-loss-chapter. Displaced anger is completely natural and will lessen as we acknowledge what has happened. However, if you ever feel your anger is motivating you to harm someone, or is becoming an obsession for revenge, you should seek immediate help.

Anger can also surface when we recall past moments of turmoil, pain or unresolved issues within our terminated relationship with the person we have lost. Suddenly we are forced to realize the reality of our separation. When that happens, memories flood through. Within these memories there are bound to be recollections of feisty exchanges, arguments and past hurts. We may over-criticize ourselves for unresolved conflicts in our past. It is unrealistic, however, to expect perfection in any relationship. Immersing ourselves in the "should haves" and "could haves" of the past will only prevent us from dealing effectively with our anger in the present, moving on, and ultimately letting go.

To understand your anger, try making a list of the "should haves" and "could haves" that you recite repeatedly to yourself. Include those you feel you personally "should have done" as well as the "should haves" and "could haves" for other people involved in your loss.

Anger also occurs when we suppress our feelings. Anger is not the most accepted emotion in today's culture. In fact, some people don't even recognize anger as part of the grieving process. Depending on our support network and situation, we may be encouraged not to show our anger. When this happens, the anger still exists and needs to be released, so it is released inward, usually with corresponding guilt. This can cause a variety of problems. We may become sick, depressed, have chronic pain or begin having nightmares. Discovering healthy ways to release our anger is important for healing.

Appropriate anger is the point that we all hope to get to eventually. In this phase we can take our anger, in whatever form, and vent it. There are many ways to release our anger appropriately. Place a checkmark next to any of the ideas below that you think would be helpful to you. Try one of these exercises the next time you find yourself upset and anger-ridden.

- Beat a pillow
- Create a sacred space where you can go and not be heard or seen to let the anger out of your system
- Use journaling to record and release your angry feelings
- Accept that anger is not bad—only staying angry is. We learn to accept that fact by feeling our anger and allowing it to pass, instead of taking root.
- Take a walk out into an unpopulated area and scream until you are exhausted

- Talk with a friend, therapist or counselor
- Have a good cry, let the tears flow

> **Hope Note:** *Choose several healthy outlets for your anger and record them in your journal.*

Of all the emotions, anger is the most difficult to deal with. We live in a society where anger is frowned upon. Anger scares people. Anger indicates that we are "out of control." Angry people are often labeled "bad people." However there is a big difference between an angry person and a person who is feeling their anger. The latter is a temporary state—not a permanent one. But, when we don't allow our anger the opportunity to pass through us, it takes hold and we experience life through an angry lens of distortion. We might be outwardly angry and loud—or we may be quietly angry. We look happy and nice most of the time—but then we give someone a little jab here or a little jab there. Or we might become bitter, which is the debilitating cousin to anger.

The question becomes: how do we honor and feel our anger in a world where anger is considered "bad"? We accept that anger is not bad—only staying angry is. We must learn to accept that by feeling our anger and allowing it to pass, we are letting it go instead of letting it take root. We must learn to make space to honor our emotions—the good, the bad and the ugly, with the hope of moving forward.

Anxiety – Anxiety is a sense of nervousness, edginess or agitation, often without a readily identifiable source. Sometimes it is attached to an event that we consider difficult or dangerous, like driving in a strange city, or facing an unknown future. We feel our heart race, our palms sweat and a general sense of unease. At its worst, anxiety turns into a panic attack where our breathing is stifled and we may feel like we are having a heart attack.

Anxiety is often accompanied by additional emotions—fear, anger, sadness—it tends to travel with a partner. When we feel anxious, the most important thing we can do is pinpoint the cause, take a deep breath and conduct a "reality check."

Begin by asking yourself, "What do I feel anxious about?" Say your answer aloud or write it down. Continue asking yourself this question until you find an answer that carries some "zing" to it. You'll know in your gut when you have stumbled on the true source of your anxiety. Often, you'll have to ask yourself this question several times to get to the true source.

Once you have uncovered the true source, write it down on a piece of paper. (If you are using the *Companion Workbook*, see the contents for a corresponding exercise.) Beneath your sentence write down the "fact and fiction" about your statement. For example, if you have written, "I feel anxious about driving in a big city because I think I will get into an accident," write down what reality supports your statement and what doesn't. If you have driven in the city before, and were not in an accident, that would be a strike against your anxiety. If you took your time, wore your seat-belt and had a good map, those would be a few more strikes against your anxiety. Continue looking for "faults" in your anxiety. This exercise can often decrease or eliminate our anxiety altogether.

Hope Note: When we feel anxious, the most important thing we can do is pinpoint the cause, take a deep breath and conduct a "reality check."

As unfair and as unjust as life can be, it always offers us a choice. Remember that 98% of what we worry about never happens. Living in a state of perpetual worry is a terrible way to live life. If you find yourself constantly riddled by anxiety, you will need an arsenal of cognitive exercises (like the aforementioned "Reality Check") to begin to loosen anxiety's hold. You may also want to consult a professional to see if you have General Anxiety Disorder. This disorder is quite prevalent in today's hectic world and there are supportive systems in place to help those who are suffering in its grip.

Bitterness – I can best describe bitterness as a shadow that will not lift. It is a cloud that casts its dark color on our every thought and action, constantly reminding us of how unjust life can be. Those of you who feel it, recognize this emotion easily. It's that abyss that is always a step away and that follows us no matter how fast we run.

Bitterness is caused by an incomplete grieving cycle. When we don't do our grief work and find conclusive meaning; when we don't accept responsibility; when we don't reconcile ourselves to our loss and relevant reality, bitterness sweeps over our life.

Some bitterness is to be expected as we work through our grief, but in the end, it should not be a predominant state in which we continue to live. Those who face each day with a "chip on their shoulder" are examples of people who have chosen to let bitterness take control.

> **Hope Note:** *As unfair and as unjust as life can be, it always offers us a choice.*

In our times of loss we have the choice to grow or to wilt. No one can make the choice for us—we are each responsible for how we choose to live our lives. It may seem impossible to choose to live a good life after the loss we have experienced. That is simply a sign that you are not far enough along in your grief work. When you grieve healthily, choosing higher ground becomes the easy choice—staying stuck the difficult one.

That doesn't mean that at the end of Step Ten life comes up roses—surely, I am not that naive. Life will always be different. Life will always be bittersweet. But life remains the greatest gift we are given, and the greatest way to accept that gift is to live it...not to fall victim to it.

Blame – Although blame is more an action than an emotion, I feel it appropriate to address here. Blame is dangerous. When we sit with blame, we give ourselves an excuse not to move forward. Everything is someone else's fault. Our pain, our sadness, our depression—it's all someone else's doing.

"If only" are two words uttered over and over again when we are stuck in the blame game. Instead of moving forward, we recount the ways our life could be different "if only" something would or wouldn't have happened. Blame becomes anger's "scape goat."

Blame is a mask. When you take it off, you often see fear. Fear to feel our emotions, fear to go inside and dig through the darkness. Or you may see anger and unforgiveness. When we feel angry we don't have to think ahead toward hope. We don't have to plan for the future— because our future remains at the hands of someone or something else.

Through blame, we can seemingly skip the parts of life we don't want to face and page forward to something else. Or we can page backward and recant the "if only's" of a past we cannot change.

When we get stuck in the blame game we halt our grief work. We can attempt to move forward but the game will always be waiting for us. Moving through blame is much like moving through anxiety.

First, we write down who we blame and for what. Sometimes we blame ourselves. No matter whom or what it is, write it down or say it aloud. (If you are using the *Companion Workbook*, please see the Blame Game exercise.)

Then write down the evidence you have to support your claim. As we do this, we quickly see whether our blame is founded or unfounded. If we find that reality does not support our blame, we can then begin to let that blame go. Each time we repeat the feeling we can dig for another fact that demonstrates its untruth. You will find several exercises for working through blame in the *Grief Steps®️ Companion Workbook*.

Sometimes, our blame is justified. Perhaps someone we loved developed lung cancer because they smoked cigarettes. We may blame them for the illness. Perhaps someone we loved was killed by a drunk driver. We may blame the person who drank. These cases have a solid argument for blame. In these cases, we need to move toward forgiveness (which we cover in detail in Step Five.) Blame, like guilt, doesn't hurt anyone but the beholder. By choosing to hold onto blame you are tightening its grip on your life. Sometimes, ironically, detachment takes the form of attachment to something else. In order to detach from our feelings and our pain, we attach ourselves to work, a hobby or a substance. We find something to occupy us other than the pain we feel inside, providing a way to avoid rather than address forgiveness.

Detachment – Detachment is another common step in our grief work. Usually when we experience the shock of our loss, we temporarily detach from the world around us. It is too hard to face our loss, so our body shuts down, blocking off reality. If we move through our grief work successfully, little by little we reopen ourselves to reality until we fully rejoin society. When we don't successfully complete our grief work, we remain in a state of detachment where we continue to withdraw from people, hobbies, events and feelings.

How can you tell if you are in a state of detachment? Have you abandoned the majority of the friends you had before your loss? If so, you are in a state of detachment. If you were asked, "How do you feel?" and could not answer, you are in a state of detachment. Have you given up hobbies you enjoyed before your loss? If yes, you are in a state of detachment—all leading to emotional withdrawal.

Life does cycle and change, and this does not mean that we should hold onto everything. Often when we experience a loss, we lose other pieces of our lives, as well. For example, if we have lost a significant relationship, we may lose friends that we used to engage with as couples. That is normal. Likewise, we may take a year or two break from an activity that was once enjoyed. That too is normal. It's when we begin withdrawing from ALL or the majority, of, specific life areas that we know we have not grieved successfully.

Why do we detach? Like many other coping mechanisms, we detach because we hope it will minimize our pain. If we don't associate with the people or events that remind us of our hurt, perhaps we can avoid our hurt all-together. However, continued detachment and emotional withdrawal will only postpone the process of healthy recovery.

Hope Note: Continued detachment and emotional withdrawal will only postpone the process of healthy recovery.

Fear - Throughout our grief work, fear can be debilitating. Some people experience fear in a small number of areas, while others become overwhelmed by fear. It is perfectly natural to be fearful. We have experienced a loss we were ill-prepared for. Common fears can include fearing any situation that remotely resembles our current loss (i.e. if we lost a relationship, we may fear losing a new relationship. We might fear that others we love will undergo similar pain— if we are suffering from an illness, we may worry our children will face the same fate). Fearing we will be unable to go on, and even fearing that the simplest activities will lead to repeated tragedy can become very common.

Fear serves several purposes. In the initial stages of grief it gives us something on which to focus besides our loss. It also offers potential control. For example, if someone we loved died in a car accident and now we fear that riding in a car could kill us, and choose not to ride in a car, we create the illusion of control. When we face a substantial loss our lives and emotions whirl out of control. At first it is common to seek any sort of control measures that we can find. Most of the time, fear will run its course naturally. If you find your fear becoming debilitating, seek the help of a professional.

Guilt – Of all the blocks mentioned in this chapter, guilt may be the strongest of all. Struggling with the question, "Why did this happen to me?" can create so much anxiety, pain and self-doubt that you stay stuck in your grief, much longer and more intensely than needed.

We must remind ourselves that our goal is to overcome, and resume a healthy lifestyle full of meaning. Guilt won't let us do that.

The causes of guilt are varied depending on the type of loss we have experienced. If we are the family breadwinner and lose our job, we may feel intense guilt about "letting our family down." We may feel that guilt is the way to "pay penance" or that intense guilt is required because of our loss.

However, we must remember that guilt is a useless motion. It's like a glue that cements us to our pain. We cannot move forward when shrouded with guilt. We must remind ourselves that our goal is to overcome this negative feeling and resume a healthy lifestyle full of meaning. Harboring guilt won't let us do that.

Process your guilt with a trusted friend, therapist, clergy person or through the journaling and releasing your feeling exercises found throughout this book.

Hatred – It's important to check for self-hatred. Often, self-hatred isn't obvious, but look a little deeper. Are you engaging in any activities that are causing you harm? Do you drink excessively, overeat (or under-eat), smoke, abuse prescription or non-prescription drugs?

Think of someone you love dearly. Would you ever knowingly hurt them? Would you try to help them if you felt they were drinking excessively, using food as a vice, abusing prescription or non-prescription medicines? If they constantly belittled themselves or threatened to harm themselves would you step in? What if they tried to "shut themselves off" from the world at large? As a true friend, you would likely try to help. We do not unknowingly let our friends go through pain. Likewise, we need to have that same love for ourselves—stepping in when we see our own self-hatred causing pain or deterioration.

When we are able to see these excesses and abuses they become signals that there is some degree of self-hatred within us. These abuses are quite common. I know I have had my share of them. These abuses are clues that we have not found the wholeness, meaning and peace that we deserve to find in this lifetime. They are also signals that we are on the wrong path. Instead of looking within, we have looked to our excesses for the peace we haven't found within ourselves.

So where does this self-hatred or self-destructiveness stem from? Why do we engage in these excesses to begin with? It is all tied back to our feelings. We live much of our life on autopilot, not in tune with our feelings from moment-to-moment. We find ourselves with feelings of anger or sadness or depression and we don't know what to do. We know we don't have the skills to cope (or at least we don't think we do). And besides, dealing with these emotions seems so "messy." Why do that when we live in a world of instant gratification? Why go through months of grief work when we can reach for a pill or a drink or a chocolate to seemingly alleviate the pain? Instead of developing that arsenal of emotional skills to deal with our feelings, we develop an arsenal of excesses to cover them up. We pile bandage upon bandage until we forget how the original wound was caused in the first place.

The process of overcoming our excesses and healing our self-hatred involves pealing back the bandages, one by one, until we expose the original wound. Then we heal the original wound. As we learn to understand, express and honor our feelings the wound begins to heal. As it does, the excesses become unneeded and begin to fall away on their own.

Have you ever tried to quit smoking or known someone who has? It can be a battle, indeed. And why is it so tough to stick with a healthy eating plan? We are trying to change a behavior without ever taking care of the wound beneath the excess. Sure, we can quit smoking or eat healthier foods, but if we don't address the wound that caused us to acquire the habit in the first place, we are likely to slip, or substitute a different excess in its place. When we work the process in reverse, taking care of the wound first, the excess and bad habits often fall away on their own accord. (Note: if you are suffering from an emotional disorder or mental illness, it may be more difficult to shed excesses. Seek the help of a professional to guide you through the process as painlessly as possible. For example, I have an active diagnosis of Obsessive Compulsive Disorder. This disorder creates special challenges when I attempt to complete traditional cognitive exercises. Understanding these unique challenges has been the best way for me to move past them.)

> **Hope Note:** *By completing the Steps within this book, you will learn how to identify your feelings. You will learn how to express them healthily and you will learn that you can become whole again. You can use these same skills to deal with any hurts from your past.*

Helplessness – Helplessness stems from not knowing our own power. When we underestimate or are detached from the miracles that we are, and the power we can exert, we feel helpless. We feel our lives moving forward and that we have little control over the process. We don't know how to cope or make decisions. We don't know how to get from Point A to Point B—sometimes we don't even know where Point A or Point B are.

Helplessness can also come from being stifled when life seems to pile one thing then another on top of us. The bigger the pile the more overwhelmed we become until our overwhelmed feelings transform to helplessness. The pile is so big, we don't know where to start. And so we don't. As we remain inactive, the pile gets bigger, further propelling our sense of helplessness.

The way out of this vicious cycle begins by realizing that we do have a choice. We always have a choice. The journey begins the day we make the choice to take the first Step. Keep in mind I wrote *step* not *leap*. We take one little step at a time, honing our skills, until we emerge from our sense of helplessness.

Hopelessness – Of all the emotions, hopelessness can be the scariest. True hopelessness involves feeling that not only is the world unjust and unfair, but that it won't and can't change. Hopelessness is where people give up. They decide that they can never feel any better and it isn't worth the effort to try. Hopelessness, like helplessness, comes when we give up our power to choose.

Fortunately, like all of these difficult emotions, there is a way out of hopelessness. It can be the hardest emotion to work with since it is so deeply rooted. Convincing ourselves to try can be very difficult.

Like other unhealthy emotions, hopelessness comes from unfinished grief work. When we don't complete the Steps to find new meaning, and to integrate our loss with our life, we become hopeless and unable to see any reason to carry on.

Hope Note: The Steps within this book can carry you through unresolved grief and show you the way out of this dark place. Take a little step... then another... then another... Yes, grief is a journey of 2000 miles, but as the Chinese proverb states, "it begins with a single step." You have already taken your first step by beginning this book. You have believed enough to read this far. Let that be the first step. Now, keep reading, let that be the next.

Loneliness – Whenever we feel the need to reach out yet no one is there to reciprocate, loneliness ensues. Sometimes our loneliness is valid—we don't have access to the specific help that we desire. At other times loneliness is caused by our own choice not to reach out to others (unhealthy detachment).

Fortunately, loneliness is one of the emotions over which we have the most control. Thanks to the variety of support groups, the internet and our own personal circles, there is always someone that we can reach out to, if we gather the energy to do so.

In the case of loss, often our loneliness is a yearning for the person or thing that we have lost. While we can't replace the exact thing or person we have lost, we can work through Step Eight to understand the void. We can minimize the pain of our loneliness with healthy steps toward healing.

Numbness – When we face loss, it often feels like the world is moving by and around us while we are standing still. We are in a fog, a haze. Life can seem almost surreal. This is a state of numbness. Numbness arrives after the shock of learning about our loss. Our body and mind continue to shut down in an attempt to protect us from the harsh reality at hand. As we do our grief work this numbness fades.

When we don't complete our grief work, numbness continues to surround us. We lose touch with our feelings as we attempt to protect ourselves from the pain. A perpetual feeling of numbness serves as a clue that we are not dealing with our emotions, feelings and losses successfully. Consequently numbness can last for a long time.

Sadness and Depression - It is important to note that there is a difference between sadness and depression. While we grieve, we should expect to feel sadness. The intensity of this sadness will differ with the type of loss we are grieving. Shedding tears and being emotional often constitute sadness—not depression. If you find yourself immobilized, unable to concentrate, sleeping too much or too little, you are grieving, You will likely experience grief and sadness through the following traits (although these should be temporary):

- weakness and feeling drained
- loss of appetite
- extreme fatigue

- extreme irritability
- unresponsiveness
- inability to focus or concentrate
- feeling hopeless or powerless
- aches and pains
- lack of personal hygiene
- a feeling that the world is not a safe place

In her book *The Courage to Grieve*, Judy Tatelbaum writes, "So much of our energy is tied up inside that little energy is available for the action of functioning. We may be moody. At times we may feel pain and weep, and then at other times we may feel detached and without emotion. During this period we may be withdrawn and unable to relate to other people. Negativity, pessimism, emptiness and a temporary sense of meaninglessness of life are all symptoms of depression. 'What's the use?' or 'Why bother?' are typical feelings. We may be acutely restless and then become immobile. The essential thing to remember is that the pain of grief is never constant and does not last forever. Throughout this middle phase of mourning, the myriad of feelings of grief come and go in waves, with lessening intensity. Any feelings we don't face will take root in our heart and color our world as time goes on."

"Lessening intensity" are the key words here. If you are progressing healthily you should notice these "symptoms" of grief subsiding. If these symptoms do not subside or begin to cause you physical or emotional harm, professional help is needed. If you are unsure if you are feeling depression or sadness, please seek the help of a professional for a diagnosis.

> **Hope Note:** *The essential thing to remember is that the pain of grief is never constant and does not last forever. Let the river of pain flow away from you, as you begin to recognize the currents of healing.*

Understanding Emotional Triggers

It is not only important to understand what emotions we are feeling, it is also important to understand how these emotions affect us. It can be helpful to keep a journal documenting your "emotional triggers."

Cognitive experts have determined that what we think about creates our feelings, our feelings create our moods and our moods fuel our actions. In its most basic sense the equation looks like this:

> Thoughts = feelings,
> which = moods, which = actions
> **therefore** *Thoughts = actions*

When we work this equation in reverse, we can see where our actions stem from. First, take an action and ask yourself what type of mood you were in when you did it. Then ask yourself what feelings led to that mood. Lastly, ask yourself what thoughts you were feeling. This process may be tenuous at first, but the more often you do it, the easier it will become. This is an excellent way to get in touch with your thoughts and feelings, and to see how they affect your life.

Once you have done this exercise a few times, you will be able to recognize "triggers." When you recognize a thought process, you will know what mood and action it will lead to. Knowing this gives you the opportunity to change your thoughts and thus change the eventual action. This process is where the cliché, "Change your mind, change your life," stems from. See the *Grief Steps® Companion Workbook* for more exercises in cognitive thinking.

Step Three: Active Grieving and Acknowledgement

Purpose: To acknowledge the reality of our loss and engage in healthy, active grieving.

"Trying to hide or escape our grief is often more painful than experiencing grief."

~ Brook Noel

As we emerge from shock's grip, more and more emotions flood forward. It often feels like a roller-coaster as we dip back and forth between emotions. Remember how in Step One we created a space to honor our emotions? We do the same in Step Three—only now we will have many more emotions to face. Our shock has begun to subside, allowing us more resources with which to confront these confusing emotions. As painful as it may be, we must face them. Look again at the list of negative emotions in the preceding chapter. Do you want those emotions to lodge in your heart and impact your world? My guess is that you do not.

Notice that I don't use the word "acceptance" as part of this Step. Few of us are willing to "accept" our loss. How can we with the void it has left within us? The good news is that we don't have to accept our loss. We don't have to like it. We don't have to put on a "Pollyanna attitude" and march through our days as if we are "just fine."

What we are aiming for is acknowledgement. We need to acknowledge the reality of the loss in our lives and the void it has left behind. We don't get over our loss, but we can adapt to the life we have now.

As I mentioned in Step One, our bodies and minds initially shelter us from the pain of our loss. As we move through the first two Steps successfully, we come to a place where we are equipped to acknowledge reality. With that acknowledgement comes the process of active grieving.

Many grievers try to bypass this Step. They don't want

to acknowledge the loss. They don't want to admit it is real. I did this as I faced the loss of my brother. I kept very busy, jumping from project to project. I immediately started authoring a book and immersed myself in anything that would help prevent facing the fact that my brother was gone. My actions only stilted my grieving. The need for acknowledgement continued to build within me causing sadness, depression and a general feeling of unease. As I formulated the Grief Steps® and worked through them, making the space to feel my grief, I was finally able to acknowledge the reality of my brother's death.

How do we acknowledge our loss? We take the emotions that are within us and move them outside of us. We quit sheltering our pain and instead we purge it into the real world. We may complete this purging by:

· Journaling our emotions and sharing them with a trusted friend.
· Joining a support group and talking to others about our loss.
· Confiding in a close friend about how we feel.
· Seeking the help of a professional and vocalizing our loss to them.
· Learning to talk about our loss with others when the subject arises.
· Joining a trusted support site like GriefSteps® (www.griefsteps.com) and sharing our story with others.

Why is it so important to share these feelings with others? When we do so we give them life, we acknowledge their reality. Think about it. We have so many thoughts that twirl in our heads. Many of our worries never happen. They are preoccupations or silly things we wouldn't vocalize. When we take a thought or feeling and express it in the real world, we give it credibility, we move it outside of ourselves and acknowledge its realness. Perhaps you can recall one of your own thinking patterns that seemed so "credible" when it existed solely in your mind. When you took this same thinking pattern (they are usually unhealthy patterns) and shared it with a trusted friend, he or she could poke many holes in it. Releasing our emotions externally, automatically gives them a "reality test." While this may not overtly create change, change is indeed occurring. We are no longer living and thinking on "autopilot," but instead with purpose. We are chipping away the barrier that grief can build within us when left untended and unmonitored. We are opening a pathway that can lead to wholeness.

In looking at active grieving and acknowledgement, it is important to examine what blocks this process. By understanding what blocks us, we can create a roadmap to remove the block.

The main reason we avoid acknowledgement is that with it comes pain. To truly feel our loss and acknowledge its realness, we must face deep-rooted sadness. We might fear that when we go into this dark place, we won't come out.

The human mind, soul and spirit, carry unique abilities. Ask many people who have survived tragedy if they ever thought they would be able to face such difficulty. Often you'll hear a resounding "no." Personally, I would have never guessed myself capable of handling the losses I have endured in my lifetime. But what happens is surprising. Our spirit yearns to survive, experience and live. Even when faced with unimaginable tragedy, our soul digs into reserves of courage that we never knew were there. It is this experience, this process, that we must trust when we engage in active grieving.

Understanding our deepest questions is an important step to complete before entering into the actual exercises. Examine your loss. What specifically is the hardest part for you to face? From what reality are you trying to escape? Know that when your grief journey takes you close to these answers you are likely to take a step back or recoil. Realize and respect what is hard for you. But then dig past it, or dig around it, so that you can move forward toward acknowledgement and release. Many people know this as "action therapy." By using action you move beyond the problem, thus dissolving the problem. You've literally "answered" and "solved" your problem through the use of action.

The first part of this chapter contains tools you can use to express your emotions. The second part of the chapter provides exercises that can help you explore your emotions and grieve in a healthy way.

I suggest trying each tool and exercise once and then creating a combination of those that are most effective for you. If you are using the *Grief Steps® Companion Workbook* see the exercises for "Facing Your Emotions" for additional ideas.

Tools for Exploration

Make A Space: If you're like me, you may find it helpful to schedule a "Vacation for Feeling." In order for me to truly get in touch with how I felt, I had to make a safe space for the feelings to surface. My day-to-day life as a CEO and Mom is hectic and crazy, and doesn't allow me a single sidestep. Only by taking several days away, with the sole intention of exposing my grief, was I then able to let my emotions rise to the surface. In the safety of a closed room, I could feel my sadness. There was no one there to see me as "weak," and no one there that I had to care for. My only "roommate" was my grief.

> **Hope Note:** *Where will you create a space for your grief?*

Develop Your Grief Sessions: "Grief Sessions" are set times when you honor your feelings. In our busy days we tend to immerse ourselves in the activities of life (sometimes mindful, sometimes mindless) leaving us little time to experience our grief. But we can't get through what we do not feel.

Some people find success in spending an hour taking a walk and getting in touch with their grief, while others can sit outside with a journal and express their feelings. Just as our grief is unique, so will our sessions be. Write down some ideas for your own Grief Sessions—then schedule one on your calendar.

Hope Note: When and where will you hold your first Grief Session? Take the time to make a concrete appointment for yourself. You are worth it.

Try Your Hand at Journaling: As I mentioned before, writing about feelings has proven a successful venue for many people. When you write, don't worry about punctuation, grammar or how your writing might sound to another person. When you are writing, just aim to express your innermost thoughts. Write whatever comes to mind. Dig for words. Anything goes when journaling. You can keep your journal or burn your pages—whatever is most comfortable for you. I recommend keeping your journal as a chronicle of your journey. However, if several pages are extremely sensitive, you may choose to burn those pages or keep them in a password protected file on a computer; or if handwritten, under lock and key. You want your journal to be a private and secure place where you can explore your feelings without concern.

The actual physical act of "writing" can be very

rewarding. It shows a respect and caring for ourselves, since we take the time to create a thoughtful page that can be held and reread. We are valuing our abstract thoughts by giving them a "physical existence." I have worked with many people who have found this process both cleansing and healing (even those people who swore they would never enjoy writing). Being able to look back on a collection of writing is encouraging—we see how far we have come.

If you have a difficult time starting to write, try listening to some emotional or moving music. Let the notes evoke your feelings and write about what you feel.

Using a sentence-starter can also be helpful. Try writing "I feel..." and then completing the sentence. Continue doing that over and over. The more times you do this, the more the sentence-starter will reveal. Or you can use a sentence-starter that names an emotion, "I feel angry because..."

Try using some of the following "starters" in your journaling. The *Grief Steps® Companion Workbook* contains additional ideas.

I am sad because...
I am angry because...
I feel anxious about....
I am depressed about...
I feel lonely when...
I am scared that....
The hardest part is...
I miss...

I regret that…
I can't handle…
I wish I…

Hope Note: *Choose two sentence-starters*
from the list above and use them in your
journaling today or tomorrow.

Try Writing Poetry: Poetry creates a bridge (of feelings) between the material world and the world of creativity and spirit. Visiting and/or joining a poetry group can have an extraordinary effect on the way we heal our grief. Poets, by definition, get to the raw feelings behind the masks we all wear. When we are wearing the mask of grief, we may feel that others cannot possibly know the pain we are experiencing, yet we must still continue living day to day in spite of our tremendous loss. As a result, we may feel out of touch with friends who have not experienced such a loss. We may feel that our strength of feeling is unacceptable to others. Feelings are the dynamic force behind poetry groups. Within these groups you will find a welcome and sensitive home for the powerful expression of your grief through using written and spoken word.

Check your local paper for poetry readings or "open mic" nights. Many bookstores and colleges conduct such events. Attend the readings and ask participants about other local events or groups in your area. The point is to dig past the surface and into your soul—and then to give your soul a space to express itself.

You can also write poetry on your own, or write it on your own and share through online poetry groups. Many books exist that can fuel creativity and offer guidance. Check the writing/reference section at your local bookstore. If you are using the *Grief Steps® Companion Workbook,* look up the additional poetry ideas. If you would like to purchase a book on poetry, I strongly recommend *POEM CRAZY: Freeing Your Life with Word* by Susan G. Wooldridge (ISBN 0609800981). Another good book is *WRITING THE NATURAL WAY: Using Right-Brain Techniques to Release Your Expressive Powers* by George Rico, PhD and Tyler Volk (ISBN 0874779618).

It can be extremely cleansing to spend a morning, once a week, at a cafe or a park, writing poetry in a beautiful journal. Don't worry about form—just creatively put down words to express yourself. One member of our Grief Steps® group had this to say about poetry:

> *"I love to read and to attempt to write*
> *poetry. I love the 'expansion' of words when*
> *they are combined in such interesting*
> *and tactile ways. Also being an artist I enjoy*
> *the 'visual effects' that words contain when*
> *used in metaphor and the simple, yet*
> *complex, message they can imply. I gain*
> *much of my inspiration from reading. One of*
> *my favorite haiku (i.e. short syllabled Japa-*
> *nese verse forms) simply states: 'Now that*
> *my house burned down—better*
> *I can see the moon.'*

*To me. this implies how undaunted our
spirit can be during crisis. Even though we
are in sorrow about what has happened, a
new perspective can be opened if we
choose…suddenly we have had an introduc-
tion to much more than just our bodies here
on earth…we have been introduced to
eternity and the universe itself. Just as our
spirit lives on, so does our loved one's. I
truly believe that we do not 'die dead' but
that we die into something greater."*

Utilize Freewriting: Freewriting is the process of
recording thoughts and feelings on the fly. Instead of
analyzing what you are writing, or worrying about form or
structure, you just write continually. There are only two
rules for freewriting—you can't stop moving your pen or
pencil—and you can't erase anything you have written. The
point of this exercise is to dig past the surface and into your
soul—and then to give your soul a space to express itself.
Freewriting works especially well for those who are
intimidated by the thought of journaling or it can also be
used in conjunction with journaling. I recommend a 5-
minute freewrite first thing in the morning. When we first
wake, we can access our innermost thoughts more readily.
If you are leery about trying a freewrite, that is all the more
reason to push yourself to do so. You might find that this can

help you uncover much of your inner life. Try to make a commitment to freewrite at least four mornings each week for five minutes. Set a timer for yourself. When the timer dings, stop writing.

> **Hope Note:** *Put down this book and try a five minute freewrite. Avoid excuses and just take action.*

Healing Old Wounds: If it has been a long time since you have experienced your loss and you are working or reworking through Step Three you may not be fully aware of all of your emotions. As mentioned before, repressed emotions and unresolved issues can lay await in dormant fashion for years, blocking your journey through healthy grieving.

All of the exercises within this book can work equally well to help you heal old wounds. However, before you attempt to heal an old wound, you must first uncover it. Uncovering the wound involves facing it again— resurrecting all the emotions that you may not have felt for a very long time. For this reason, you may want to consider a support group or professional to guide you through this process. If you choose to do this on your own, make sure to re-familiarize yourself with the "Self-Checks" mentioned in the early sections of this book.

Before turning to the exercises, stir long dormant emotions by looking at old pictures or reading items that you associate with your loss. You may want to try "reliving the day" that you learned of your loss. It may help to relive other days as well to get in touch with more emotions. Some significant-day examples might include: the day of a funeral, the day a divorce was finalized or the day belongings were moved from a home, a cross-country move where friendships were lost, or the death of a favorite childhood pet. Think of the activities and interests, people and places you have avoided since your loss. Revisit one or two to re-experience the waves of emotion you once felt. As someone who has repressed grief in the past, I understand how illogical it may seem to go back and "look for grief" when your day-to-day life has become relatively painless. But let me ask you this, is your day-to-day life complete? Is there happiness in your heart? Or is there a sense of sadness, hopelessness, or maybe just an ache? Have you become numb? We can't heal our hearts without dealing with the source of the symptom and the source is often found by revisiting unresolved grief.

There is an old saying, "You can't go home again." While it is true that we cannot return to the place we once new as "home," where we were free from the pain of grief, we can revisit with a new perspective. When we heal old wounds that is precisely what we are doing. We are going back and looking at our experiences from a fresh perspective. We are exploring the depth of our feelings and finding the tools to move forward from the very experience we tried to leave behind.

Hope Note: When we heal old wounds, we engage in a process of going back and looking at our experiences from a fresh perspective. We are exploring the depth of our feelings and finding the tools to move forward from the very experience we tried to leave behind.

Identify Your Emotions: One of the most valuable skills we can gain during the grief journey is the ability to identify and understand our emotions. When we feel a gnawing sense of pain, we need to ask ourselves… "How do I feel?" With emotions buried or repressed, we often just know we feel "bad" but are unsure why. When we don't understand our feelings, it's like going to the doctor seeking treatment for pain, but when the doctor asks why we are there our response is… "Something hurts, but I'm not sure what." We could spend hours going back and forth to the doctor, but without an identified cause of the pain, and a clear diagnosis, the odds of successful treatment aren't good. Doctors ask us questions to help isolate and identify our pain. Once determined, a treatment can be selected. Grief work is very similar. We need to ask ourselves questions and identify our emotions so that we can "treat" them.

The next time you feel a gnawing pain, ask "What am I feeling?" Continue to ask this question of yourself, journaling your answers, until you stumble across the answer that feels intuitively "real." After you identify your feeling, you can then move to the appropriate Grief Step or exercise to help you understand and "treat" the pain.

Exercises for Active Grieving

Living for Today: Many times after we experience loss we wish we would have had more time to experience life as we once knew it. Loss is inevitable. We will experience many more losses in our lives and lose things we currently hold precious. Those who move through grief work naturally come to share one predominating trait—they live in the moment. Their list of regrets is short, because they make the most of each day. Many times, after experiencing loss, we learn, perhaps for the first time, how precious "a moment" can be. We learn how temporary and fluid our world is. Living for today can help you honor your grief by finding something "good" in the rubble. It can also help you have less regrets and guilt should you experience more loss in your future.

Hope Note: Write a couple pages in your journal about how you can live more in the moment. Also take a moment to appreciate all the current blessings in your life—great and small.

Let Loose: Throughout our grief work, we continually focus on how to transform what has happened into a meaningful pathway toward the future. Sometimes, it's tiring to be optimistic, to be hopeful—to want to look for that silver lining. Set aside an hour to write about all that has gone wrong. Write about what is unfair and unjust. Don't look for the bright side—just purge all the stuffed-up feelings onto paper. Let loose. Let the negativity go.

For Relationships—Recognize the Good and the Bad: Relationship expert Sherry Amatenstein suggests that people "write a relationship profit and loss statement." There are things we can uncover about ourselves at the end of a relationship that we may not see at other periods in our lives. Amatenstein suggests we, "Look at your assets. For example, the ability to really be there for someone in a crunch. Examine the minuses—perhaps you were too trusting of someone who hadn't earned it. The bottom line: analyze what was right and wrong about your old relationship."

By identifying the positive and negative aspects of our loss, we can identify what we have the ability to change as we move forward.

The Serenity Prayer: In *Chapter Two, The Emotional Rollercoaster,* we covered blame in depth. Through blame, we attempt to gain control of the noncontrollable. It's amazing how we will fight for control—even to our own detriment. Relinquishing the illusion of control can be frightening. So much of life's unhappiness stems from trying to exert power over things we are powerless to control. When we learn to quit focusing our energies on the unchangeable, and instead focus on where we can be effective, we take a large step on the pathway to peace. The Serenity Prayer so beautifully summarizes this point,

> God grant me the Serenity
> to accept the things I cannot change;

Courage to change the things I can;
and Wisdom to know the difference.

~Reinhold Neibuhr

This prayer is one we would all do well to practice daily. When we truly understand what we cannot change, and face the things we can with courage, we relieve stress, unease and unhappiness. Read the Serenity Prayer several times, slowly. What are the images that come to your mind when you read this? Write about the things that you have tried to control, that you now realize are out of your control. How does it feel to let those go and accept that you cannot change them? Write about the things that you can control. How can you face them with courage? I suggest copying this prayer onto an index card or two and putting it where you will see it often. In the *Grief Steps® Companion Workbook* you'll find this printed on a pocket reminder card along with other cards that carry valuable messages for your journey.

Realize Your Resilience: When we face loss, it can be of help to remember other times in our past when we have faced loss, and have come out okay. Even if the events were small or seemingly insignificant, they were still training and conditioning, that evidence the resilience of the human spirit. In a sense, we experience many "mini-deaths" throughout our lifetime, or as Judith Viorst calls them, "necessary losses." We separate from our parents; we lose our freedom to play, in turn for work and accountability. We lose our childhood, baby teeth, myths (such as Santa Claus), wisdom teeth. As we age we lose our youth, health, dexterity, mental awareness, eye sight. We lose weight when we diet. We lose our parents, grand parents, pets, friends. We might lose our homes, our jobs, our children to college and marriage. Loss is a natural conclusion to so many of our life experiences.

Write about the losses you have experienced and try to recollect how you felt during the loss. Write as vividly as you can. Then write about the process of overcoming that loss and how you feel now, when looking back. Personally, I find this a great way to gather strength. There have been times in my life when I truly thought I was experiencing life's worst pain. I can remember in the moment thinking… "If I can get through this, I can get through anything." I remember how hopeless life felt—yet I pushed forward. And now my life is so rich—a richness I never would have uncovered had I not forged forward. That's not to say there won't be problems. Life will always be filled with unexpected turmoil. However, I have gathered a new strength for facing this turmoil.

> *"I think we all have a tendency to shrink back during grief (especially in the beginning), somehow hoping that the pain will lesson…that the monster of grief will somehow not find us, or overlook us, if we hide good enough. But it doesn't seem to work that way…isolation and 'solitary confine-*

ment' can be devastating. No matter how difficult it is to do so, I think we must reach out to each other to find solace and hope."
~From a Grief Steps® Member

Make a Space for Breaks: We cannot be wrapped inside our grief work, 24/7. We need a break to recoup, to regenerate, to gather our strength and face the "next wave." Lose yourself in an activity. Go see a funny movie. Take a walk. Read a book. Find some momentary means of healthy escape from your grief.

Positives and Negatives: Sometimes taking a basic look at the pros and cons of facing our grief can help us gather the motivation to move forward. Explore the negative aspects behind not handling your grief. For example, when we suppress our grief and choose not to face it, we may be angry, easily irritable, impatient, sad, missing moments of joy and even depleted of faith... make your own list of pros and cons.

It's Okay to Laugh: In Jacquelin Mitchard's novel, *The Deep End Of The Ocean*, there is an incredible scene. The book is about a family whose son has been kidnapped. The mother, Beth, is sitting in the office of the chief detective, Candy. The two women have become quite friendly throughout the weeks spent on the search. The mother has been grim, depressed and withdrawn throughout the search. In the scene, the detective says something that causes the mother to laugh. She laughs only for an instant, before a look of horror comes over her face—horror, that in the face of misery she laughed. Here is an excerpt from the scene:

> Candy held up the mailer. "Actually it's a padded cry for help."
>
> And Beth, to her horror, laughed, instantly covering her eyes and feeling that she was about to choke. Candy was on her feet and around the desk in seconds.
>
> "Beth, Beth, listen," she said. "You laughed. You only laughed. If you laugh that doesn't mean that's a point against our side. If you laugh, or read a book to Vincent, or eat something you like, it's not going to count for or against us on the big scoreboard of luck." Beth began to cry. "You have to believe me," Candy went on. "It feels like if you watch a movie, or listen to a song... that little moment of happiness is the thing that's going to be punished..."

While this scene details the events surrounding a kidnapping, many of us can relate to these feelings. At times, it's hard to laugh—we feel guilty for "going on." We wonder if our laughing makes our grief less real—if our memories will fade—if people will think we don't miss the deceased.

Multiple Grief

Some people have multiple situations they are dealing with on top of their grief. Perhaps an elderly parent is ill, you are sending a child off to college, you are going through menopause, or a career change, or completing college or some other challenging life situation. Or perhaps you have not fully grieved another past primary loss. These multiple situations can halt, delay or complicate the primary grieving process. When we have many stressful experiences, much of our emotional energy is funneled into each stressor. We are left with little reserve. Yet, in order to heal we must find a way to cope with these stressors, while still feeling and exploring our primary grief.

Although one experience may stand out in your mind, any other times of loss are likely to be important as well. Even things that might seem small or insignificant in the face of tragedy can complicate the grieving process when they accumulate. Soon we find ourselves stuck in a web of turmoil, unable to unravel our complicated feelings. Many events have mixed together and we can't pull on a single string to undue the knot—instead a tug on a single string just makes the knot tighter.

To work through multiple grief, it is important to recognize each of the experiences that you are grieving. Once you have identified those components you can begin to focus on healing. Take your time in identifying these issues—they may not come to the surface at first. If you find that you are still facing acute grief after a long period, you may want to come back to this exercise. Sometimes we suppress other losses that get caught up in the web. For example, a loss you are facing now might remind you of the absence of a parent during a difficult period in your life. Although this may not have been a death, it is a loss, and losses (not only deaths) are what lead to the experience of Multiple Grief.

The actual losses, and our reactions to them, influence how profound and intense our Multiple Grief becomes. If we have lost several family members in a car accident, we are forced to face all the emotions of grief for each family member simultaneously. Or in a situation like the Columbine tragedy, many children lost multiple classmates and friends. We know all too well how difficult dealing with grief is for one loss—it is easy to realize how each loss serves as a multiplier of our intense pain. Yet, the process for dealing with grief remains the same. The only difference is that we must recognize each experience we are grieving, and grieve each loss fully. We can expect our healing work to take longer, since we must complete each Step with regard to each loss. A support group, therapist or pastor can be especially helpful when facing Multiple Grief. When we are exhausted or overwhelmed by emotion, our support person can provide a valuable shoulder to lean on and simple words of encouragement to help us "catch our breath" and continue down the pathway of healing.

Coping with Guilt

If you are suffering from the "if onlys" or the "I should haves," and you are left with a deep feeling of regret over your loss, try the following exercise:

Try writing at least a one page letter to your loss. Tell your loss whatever you want but remember to include the following:

- the facts of what happened
- how you feel about what happened
- how this loss has affected your life

Now, turn the page over and imagine this loss "responding" to your letter. Asking questions of your loss will make this exercise extremely valuable. So write down such questions as, "How do you feel about what happened?" and "Will you please forgive me for _____?" "Have I been punished enough for my part (real or imagined) in all of this and is there anything else I can do to show you how sorry I am?" "How can I show you how much I have suffered?" Then close your eyes and answer each question as if the loss was speaking through you.

If you find this is a difficult exercise to do on your own you may want to ask a therapist or trusted friend to sit quietly with you. **Caution:** If you are being "told" by your inner voice to hurt yourself in any way, seek professional help immediately.

Hurtful Self-Talk

Hurtful self-talk can block the grieving process—keeping you stuck. Sometimes it's easier to play "negative tapes" in our mind than to move through our pain toward healing. The healing process is tough—but there is a light at the end. Overcoming hurtful self-talk is an important step toward that light.

When you find yourself running on the treadmill of hurtful self-talk it is important to come up with a positive statement for balance. Write down your destructive or hurtful thought and then write down a more positive, realistic thought. For example, "The deceased wouldn't want me to grieve," is hurtful. You could write, "The deceased would understand and respect the full spectrum of my emotions." Whenever a negative thought enters your mind, replace it with a positive, more realistic statement. Try "reprogramming" your hurtful self-talk by utilizing your journal or the *Companion Workbook*. Continue to add statements along with their positive counterparts as they occur to you throughout your journey.

Instant Replay

One of the horrors of instant replay is the persistent questioning of the choices we made. *Were there warning signs that I missed? Could I have done anything at all to prevent this loss?* This kind of constant replay, over an extended period of time, blocks acceptance and closure.

Instant replay is the mind's way of coming to terms with the unfathomable. Some instant replay is necessary, but too much can keep us stuck. If your own instant replay is becoming an obsession, make an effort to do what therapists call "thought stopping." This is a technique whereby you consciously stop the thought, and deliberately change the subject. This is not a complicated task and is easier to do than you might think.

If you replay the buildup to your loss like a bad movie, first acknowledge the sadness, then try shifting to a positive image. Replace one image with the other.

Paul G. Stoltz, Ph.D., writes in his book entitled, *Adversity Quotient: Turning Obstacles into Opportunities*, "Arm yourself with STOPPERS. Whenever a crisis strikes, anxiety is a frequent—and useless—response. It also spreads like an emotional wildfire making it impossible to apply rational steps to better cope with the problem. Soon you start to 'catastrophize' and feel helpless and hopeless. You squander energy and time worrying. To avoid imagining the worst will happen, use what I call 'stoppers' to regain control."

He continues, "When you feel overwhelmed, slap your knee or any hard surface. Shout, 'Stop!' The sting will shock you into a more rational state. Some people leave a rubber band around their wrist. When they feel anxiety, they stretch it six inches and let it go.

"Focus intently on an irrelevant object, such as a pen, the pattern of the wallpaper or a piece of furniture. If your mind is removed from the crisis, even for a moment, you can return with the calm you need to take effective action.

"Take an activity break. Just 15 or 20 minutes of brisk walking or other exercise will clear your mind, raise your energy and flood your brain with endorphins—chemicals that put you in a more optimistic mood.

"Put yourself in a setting where you're dwarfed by your

surroundings. Catastrophizing makes problems larger than life. A shift in perspective will cut them down to size. Drive to the beach and look out over the ocean...stand at the base of a large tree...gaze up at the clouds...or listen to a great piece of music and let the grandeur wash over you."

Can We Grieve Too Much?

While it is important to face our grief and move through it, there is a danger in grieving "too much." Some people get stuck in their grief, and wrap themselves in the process without the goal of moving forward. The process of grief becomes comforting, a way to link themselves to their loss.

Some people find themselves longing for any link to their loved one, even if it is painful. It is not uncommon for bereaved persons to fear they will forget their loved one's smile, or how they look, or sound, or walked. Instead of working through the process of letting go, they hold onto everything they can, scared to let the slightest memory slip away.

Dr. Forest Church, author of *LIFELINES: Holding on (and Letting Go)* points out that, "Once the death of another person [or our loss] becomes an excuse for not going on with one's own life, or not being able to live fully and abundantly, then that's pathological."

When we use our loss as an excuse to hide in our past, we are entering a pathological state which demonstrates the need to go back and make sure we have completed each of the Grief Steps®.

To Go On

You can shed tears that he is gone,
Or you can smile because he lived.
You can close your eyes and pray that he will come back,
or you can open your eyes and see all he's left.
Your heart can be empty because you can't see him,
or you can be full of the love you shared.
You can turn your back on tomorrow and live yesterday,
or you can be happy for tomorrow because of yesterday.
You can remember him and only that he's gone,
or you can cherish his memory and let it live on.
You can cry and lose your mind,
be empty and turn your back,
or you can do what he'd want:
smile, open your eyes, love and go on.

> *~Author Unknown*

Step Four: Understanding Your Story

Purpose: To find a beginning, middle and end so that we may cease obsessive thinking and move beyond the story of our loss toward healing.

"Essential grief is a tearing down and then building back up..."

~ **Ashley Davis Prend,** TRANSCENDING LOSS

Whether we realize it or not, our brain is like a computer, operating a million programs. The most common program we know is that of the "cyclical story." We are used to things having a beginning, a middle and an end. For example, boy meets girl, boy and girl marry, boy and girl grow old together. Or the most basic example: human is born, human grows from childhood to adulthood, human moves through old age, human dies.

Another common program is "cause and effect." We know the earth rotates, therefore creating seasons and different temperatures. We know that when we put our hand on a stove, we will be burned. We expect that if we work hard, we will be rewarded. These are all cause and effect examples.

When we experience loss, we often experience the disruptions of these cycles. Our expectations are jarred. Our story becomes flawed. The life we find ourselves in is not the life we had bargained for. Logan, a forty-eight-year-old businessman, experienced this disruption when he lost his job as the Chief Executive Officer of a NASDAC-traded, technology company. After fifteen years in business and ten years as CEO, Logan was let go without warning in a company down-sizing. Overnight he went from an elite and privileged world to a poor economy where jobs were scarce. After eight months, he had not found employment and worries about becoming under-employed just to keep his family above water. They have already put their dream home up for sale as the mortgage payments that seemed so small have now become insurmountable to the six-member-family.

This certainly isn't the life that Logan dreamed of when he received his Masters in Business. He assumed he would continue in his power position until retirement, and then reap the rewards of his stock holdings. Instead, he is facing a career change and lifestyle change at forty-eight that contradicts all the things he has held dear in his adult life. When I met Logan, he was still in shock that his life had changed so drastically without warning. The more he tried to "get on top of things" the more he felt he was sinking. He spent hours recounting the great deeds and accomplishments he had performed in his professional life. He would finish all these stories the same way—his head in his hands, tears on his face, wondering what had happened and how he had gotten "here."

What I expressed to Logan, as I do everyone who is experiencing loss, is that we need to understand what has happened as much as possible. We need to fact-find and uncover a beginning, middle and end so that we can quit the relentless questioning that keeps us from moving forward. As I helped Logan do this, he realized that had he not "understood his story" he would have spent many more months cycling and questioning the past—all while continuing to sink in the present. In order to keep his family afloat, he had to move forward—and so much of moving forward depends on finding your beginning, middle and end. Until you have established that sequence in your mind and heart, you will be stuck in a state of constant cycling. You may find you think obsessively about your loss. Some people describe it as "living on instant replay."

Our mind keeps coming back to our loss attempting to resolve the story to fit into its "program." Until our mind has the answers it needs, it cannot move forward to deal with the next task. If we don't hunt down our beginning, middle and end we are sentencing ourselves to staying stuck.

Of course, we may not want to know our story. Afterall, this isn't the story that we dreamt about while playing dress-up as children. We drew pictures of castles and fairy tales, not pain and loss. But as we know all too well, life is not a fairy tale. Whether we want it or not, we have a story that has landed in our lap. And it's in our best interest to unravel that story and discover its pieces.

> **Hope Note:** *You have a story that only you can tell. You have lessons that you have learned, feelings that you have felt, moments that have moved you.*

In her book *Writing to Heal the Soul,* author Susan Zimmerman says, "It is a story that has torn your heart into pieces, and it is a story of beauty, because your heart couldn't have been torn without your having first loved and somehow lost something that you loved. Now is the time to begin honoring your story. A friend sent me a note that said simply, 'Blessed are the cracked, for they shall let the light in.'"

The need to 'solve the story' explains why it is so natural (and so necessary) to talk with others about our loss. Over and over again, grievers tell their stories, attempting to make sense of them, attempting to understand the cycle.

Often, there are many ways to collect information. When we have enough clues we can piece together a story that will allow our questioning to lessen. As our questions lessen, we create more room to heal. If we find ourselves reluctant to complete the exercises to understand our story, that is a signal that we are fighting the reality of our loss. Chances are more work is needed with the first three Grief Steps®.

Dr. Ann Kaiser Stearns, author of *Coming Back: Rebuilding Lives After Crisis and Loss* offers the following suggestions: "Make a conscious effort to identify what is not making sense to you about your loss or crisis. You might ask yourself: What is it about the situation… that is most puzzling or troubling to me? What part of grief is troubling me? What other things are troubling me?"

Before beginning the journey to understand your story, ask yourself the three questions Dr. Stearns suggests:

> 1. What is it about the situation that is most puzzling or troubling to me?
> 2. What part of grief is troubling me?
> 3. What other things are troubling me?

Explore your thoughts in your journal or in the *Grief Steps® Companion Workbook*.

The need to find a beginning, middle and end ties into all types of loss. I found it especially needed as I struggled to make sense of my brother's death. At the age of 27 he had been stung by a bee and died within the hour—without any history of allergy.

My mother and I had never heard of the term profound anaphylactic shock—we couldn't even pronounce it. Our initial disbelief was so strong, not a single question was asked at the hospital. But as the days went by, the questions came one after the other. Caleb had been stung a month before— was this a cumulative effect of venom? Several years prior he had suffered from chest pains that went undiagnosed— could his death be connected to that? Had any blood been drawn and a firm allergic reaction determined? If his death certificate said 12:54 and his friends said he was unconscious at 11:15—what happened between then and 12:54?

I did as much research as I could and then I called the doctor. I immediately put him at rest by letting him know that I trusted he had done everything in his capacity, and that I did not, in any way, question his ability. I let the doctor know that my questions were more about figuring out the order of events. We talked for close to an hour.

After combining his comments with my research, I was able to confidently assume that Caleb did die from a fatal reaction to a bee sting. He was dead before the ambulance arrived, or minutes after, and unconscious long before that. He was not pronounced dead until 12:54

because even doctors hope for miracles. Being so young and healthy, they worked extensively on him in the E.R. trying anything they could to revive him.

I also was able to learn that bee allergies are typically not hereditary. However, I also learned, those who know they are allergic can carry an Epinepherine shot, that can possibly reverse or delay the reaction, allowing more time to get to medical treatment.

With this knowledge and for my own peace of mind, I went to a specialist in the allergy field. I asked the allergist to test both my three-year-old daughter and myself. He took our blood and sent it to the Mayo clinic for analysis. The tests came back negative. Yet, since this allergy can develop at any time, he gave us both Epipen® kits so that we would feel more at ease. While statistically only 40 to 60 people a year die from fatal reactions to insects, it was important for me to have the comfort of preparedness.

Loss of an Intimate Relationship

Knowing the beginning, middle and end is especially important if your loss is that of an intimate relationship. There are many times where a relationship ends—only we aren't ready to let it go. We might still deeply love someone who has told us they don't love us anymore, or cannot be there for us in the capacity we would like. When we lose someone to death—we know that the loss is permanent, but if we lose someone who is living—we may be tempted to "hold on," or try to "change" or "reverse" the present circumstances.

When an important relationship ends, we can quickly become obsessive in our thinking and our sadness. We search and dig for missed clues, missed opportunities and second chances. Sometimes we find them. More often we do not.

Some people spend years holding onto a relationship that is over—trying to resuscitate something that has long faded. At the core of this obsessive seeking and seemingly endless pain is rejection. Nothing cuts a person deeper than the perception of being rejected. *What did I do? Why did this end? What's wrong with me? How can I change?* We torture ourselves with endless questioning and mind games. We look for ways we could have acted differently in an attempt to regain control of the situation. Sometimes we even try to become someone we are not.

Often as we succumb to these obsessive cycles, we end up driving the person we long for even further away. We may feel crazy, isolated, hopeless—until one day we don't even recognize our own reflection in the mirror.

To overcome and move past this obsessive cycling, we need to separate ourselves from the relationship that has ended. Relationships end for many reasons—most of which have nothing to do with personal inadequacy. People change. Life changes. Circumstances change. There are so many life forces outside of our control, and when we put ourselves in the center as the cause of a breakup, we are actually taking a very egotistical stance. Odds are the ending of the relationship had little to do with personal flaws, and everything to do with the cards life dealt.

A close friend of mine is a very professional and attractive woman. She is kind, warmhearted, generous, funny and caring. While on vacation, she met someone and connected in a way she had never before known. The two became inseparable, quickly fell in love, and had the magnetism that most couples only dream about. To everyone outside their relationship, it looked as if they were meant to be. Inside the relationship my friend and her partner felt the same way. Having both known the pain of a failed marriage, they frequently talked of how their union would be different and swore to never let their love fade.

Yet, the two lived in different cities, miles apart. They were only able to see each other every month but they talked and e-mailed daily. The passion and intensity of their relationship fueled when they were together. They traveled to exotic places, ate at the best restaurants and showered each other with gifts. They would stay up late into the night making love, laughing and sharing their dreams. Unfortunately, these short-lived "get-togethers" weren't representative of day-to-day life.

After almost a year, my friend found that he was calling less and less and seemingly pulling back from the relationship. The ease of their exchanges seemed to vanish and their reunions had longer spaces between them. My friend was devastated. She truly felt that this man was the love of her life and she wondered how this could happen. For several years after he ended the relationship, she fought to keep in touch. She yearned to "uncover" some magical reason things had changed and find a way back to the way they once were. She yearned for the intense love and passion they had once shared. I remember one night she sat and questioned, "We swore we'd love each other forever—what happened?"

While I, and my friend, will likely never know exactly what changed in her relationship, much of it looks like "life had other plans." Although the two shared an incredible love and chemistry, for whatever reason it could not withstand the distance. Instead of working through her grief, my friend halted her life, entered a deep depression and spent years trying to contort herself and her reality to get back to a place that was now in the past.

Although many relationships end for a specific reason—someone is unfaithful, passion dies, someone is abusing a substance or their partner—most relationships I have seen are like my friend's and end for other reasons. Life just changes. We have a choice when this happens. We can attempt to contort and control an uncontrollable outcome, which leads to depression and sadness, or we can stop the cycling and work through our grief. So how do we break the cycle of torment?

Reality Check

Write down everything you can about why the relationship ended. What did the other person tell you? What obstacles were created by circumstance? What influence did timing have? Next, write down what your inner-self is telling you. Write down the inadequacies that you feel. Re-read both—which statements ring true? (If you are in a depression you may need a friend to help you complete this exercise objectively.) Chances are you will see that although your inner self is blaming you—there were other circumstances that carried more weight.

Why do we blame ourselves? The answer is quite simple. If we break something, we think we can fix it. Trying to fix it offers the illusion of control. If the relationship ends due to something outside of our control—then we have no choice but to let it go. The pain of letting go is so hard that we choose instead, to let ourselves suffer, contorting the facts to crucify ourselves in search of hope, within our non-fixable situation. For others, being stuck-in or clinging to a failed relationship inhibits even the courage to leave or face change—causing needles years of suffering.

One other important component of the "realty check" is to compare what is in your mind with what exists, or actually existed. The friend I mentioned earlier has finally grieved her lost love successfully and has moved into a new relationship. One evening we were discussing her past relationship over dinner. She shared that many of the things she missed most about this man weren't actually qualities he possessed. Instead, they were qualities her mind had associated with him. Truth be told, when she looked back, she realized their conversations were quite shallow, with him having little to contribute. He also had a temper that would flare from time to time, and left extremely uneasy.

In her quest to experience only the good feelings, she had overlooked the negative aspects of the relationship. Often our desired feelings blindside us to the actualities of reality. Although painful, letting go of a loss is less painful than living in an unrecognized, perpetual state of loss, filled with false hopes and promises.

Clinging to false hopes is often seen in children of divorce. Unable to accept an uninvolved parent, children cling to their hopes of what a mother or father "should" be. It usually takes second, third, fourth and fifth failed "should bes "before a child begins to understand the reality of an uninvolved parent.

Why is it so difficult for us to face reality, even when the facts are lined up before us? Because it isn't the reality we want, or the reality we feel we deserve.

No child wants an uninvolved parent. An abused woman (or man) doesn't want to truly acknowledge that the person who should be their life partner is slowly stealing their spirit. No parent wants to face the reality that their child has become uncontrollable through drugs or alcohol and that there is little left they can do. When reality is too painful to face, it is very common for people to distort it, or try to soften it with false hope.

What is even more interesting is our ability to convince ourselves that these distortions are true. This accounts for two people having a completely different retelling of the same event. They both "swear" that their version is correct. They have both perceived reality differently. So how do we know what is real? We gather all the facts we can, and by facts, I mean information that cannot be skewed. We place all the facts next to each other and interpret the event based on this information—much like the legal system.

One might wonder: Why don't more people conduct reality checks in their lives? I think that deep in our hearts, many of us know that our version of reality won't stand a factual checking. What does that leave us? It will likely free us from old pain and resentments, but it also leaves us without a map. We knew how to operate within "our reality." If we find that our reality is skewed, we must give it up and begin walking a new path. The longer we have clung to a false reality, the harder that path is to walk.

On the flipside, people may create realities to reinforce self-limiting beliefs, and experience not only the loss of a relationship, but also a loss of self-esteem. One particular woman comes to mind. Becky had been gorgeous as a teenager, popular and well-liked among peers. Shortly after high-school she became involved in a monogamous relationship that would last for over a decade. The man she was involved with was emotionally abusive, and her fragile self-esteem took a turn for the worst. Throughout the relationship, she gained over 60 pounds and her self-worth plummeted. Eventually, she gathered the strength to leave the relationship.

After living in this negative environment for so long, many of her perceptions about relationships, men and herself became skewed. Anyone who would meet her would think she was attractive, yet her self-worth and confidence were virtually destroyed. As she attempted to enter new relationships, her low-esteem became problematic. When a man she was interested in didn't call at a confirmed time, she would overanalyze the situation and convince herself it was because she was unworthy, unattractive and unloved. Many times, her theories were disproved—with something as simple as a traffic jam or an un-charged cell phone, that kept her caller from phoning on time. Despite evidence to the contrary, her negative belief system remained solid, a forcefield around her heart. She skewed reality to fit the mold of her personal belief system.

Sometimes, we aren't ready to face reality. Instead, we have to gather more information to "make sure" we cannot have the reality we want. I faced this in my relationship with my father. My parents divorced shortly after my birth. Throughout my childhood, my mother was the anchor I could lean on, while my father was the sailboat, drifting in and out of my life at his convenience. I yearned for stability in my relationship with my father. I asked him to write once a month or call. He promised he would. He did not. There were many a conversation where I cried when I spoke to him, practically begging for his love. Yet the love that I needed was a love he could not give.

When I was fifteen, I moved across the country, switching high schools, to be closer to him and try to build a relationship. Although we got closer for a few months, he then announced he would be leaving the country to sail and conduct charters in the Virgin Islands. Once again I found myself yearning for calls and communications that never came. Recently, he has re-entered my life. I have very few expectations,

The lack of a father figure and his come-and-go parenting style, created an intense fear of abandonment in my life. It also greatly inhibited how I dealt with men in both personal and professional matters. In order to overcome this "negative hold," I had to come to terms with who my father *really* is, even if that's not the father that I *really* need.

This process did not happen overnight. Instead, it began from an accumulation of facts. Eventually, I could not ignore the fact that when I reached out my hand, there was no hand to hold. The facts were numerous and irrefutable. The facts were my reality, even though I did not like them.

Little did I know that I would use a version of what would become these very Grief Steps® to forgive, let go and move on in my late teens. The process began by acknowledging my reality. Understanding and cycling through my many emotions, facing the "if onlys"—all were needed to successfully grieve the father I wanted, but would never have. Forgiveness, which is the topic of the next chapter, played a very large role as well.

I believe that at some point in our life, we all skew our reality—sometimes for good, sometimes for bad. Either way, we are deceiving ourselves. In order to "let go" we must first have a realistic accounting of the actual event or situation of which we need to let go. That realistic accounting is the goal of the reality check. Scrutinize your own situation to make sure you are viewing your experience in its entirety.

Hope Note: *Fully understanding and acknowledging your loss will help you to move forward and let go.*

Finding Your Answers

Once you have completed your reality check, it is time to discover your beginning, middle and end. Many times relationships end for a variety of reasons. The reasons build up over time and often aren't perfectly clear. As a partner in that relationship, you have the right to get your questions answered. You have the right to your story.

In the case of a failed marriage, if you are on talking terms with your ex-partner this can be a very useful exercise. Begin by identifying the questions that you have by using the exercises throughout this chapter. Then place a call and ask to meet in a neutral territory (like a coffee shop or for lunch). Avoid territories where old feelings could easily rekindle and lead to more complications (like a late dinner with wine). Thank your ex-partner for meeting with you and explain what your goal is for the meeting. Then tactfully ask your questions. Don't judge, fight back or attempt to justify your position and don't attempt to minimize or judge their position. Remember, you are here to get THEIR answers, not express YOUR opinion. Although this restraint might be difficult, it will only benefit your understanding in the long run. Remember as one door closes, a new one is opened.

It is important to be tactful when approaching your ex-partner. Make sure there is time to talk. Ask questions inquisitively, not defensively. Explain that you are trying to move forward, but you need help—you need some answers so you can quit blaming yourself. Many ex-partners will hate to see you in pain and be more than happy to answer endless questions to help you find your way out of the haze.

If your ex-partner is unwilling or unable to talk to you, try speaking with a trusted friend of the opposite sex—perhaps someone who thinks similarly to your ex. Explain the story of the relationship and the questions you are having.

Often another viewpoint can help us to see things we may not notice on our own.

Although this example focuses on ex-partners in a failed relationship, this analytical approach also works for estranged parents, past friends and any other loss that involves two living people.

How Our Story Encourages Acknowledgement

Discovering our story, plays an important part in acknowledging all types of losses. Micki McWade, author of *Daily Meditations for Surviving A Separation, Breakup and Divorce,* and *Getting Up, Getting Over, Getting On: 12 Steps to Divorce Recovery* says, "It is natural and even necessary to go over, relive and examine the events that preceded the loss. *Is there something that could have been done differently? If I had done this or that, could the loss have been prevented?* We cannot believe at first that we are powerless over the circumstances. We just can't believe he or she is gone and we struggle against that reality for awhile. While we are in this state, our lives do become unmanageable. It may be difficult to maintain even mundane day to day activities.

"It's important to realize that we cannot control another adult human being or some events. We may influence another by good example or by reason, but we cannot make a person do what we want them to. We may be unsatisfied with the reactions of others around our loss. We may suffer disappointment and feel abandoned. If we choose to focus on these ideas, our lives become unmanageable and sad. It's so much more productive to place our attention in areas that can support and enhance our existence.

"After the acceptance of the loss, we can then begin to reassemble ourselves to adapt to the new configuration. We realize that while we don't have the power to change what has happened, we do have the power to change our own lives. This is where our true power lies—in creating our own lives. It may not seem possible in the early stages, but the power lies within us to make our existence pleasant or unpleasant, stimulating or boring, lonely or filled with relationships. We can choose to withdraw or reach out, be creative or to be stagnate. These are the things we CAN manage."

Talking to others will help you get the information you need to find your own beginning, middle and end. This information-gathering can be a major catalyst in moving past the grief of "what happened?" to the process of rebuilding. It allows the mind to cycle through the event in its entirety, instead of stopping to question and getting lost in the who, what, when, where, why and how.

Recording Your Story

You have a story that only you can tell. Sharing it with others not only helps you, but also helps others with similar losses. By doing so, you can find the information and support you need to develop your own conclusions and put an end to being stuck in debilitating grief.

Uncovering the components of your story can be done through the following exercise. Take a page in your journal and divide it into three columns (or if you are using the *Companion Workbook*, see the matching exercise). Label the columns, BEGINNING, MIDDLE and END. Write what you know for certain about each of these areas. Then write down the questions you have. Over the course of the next few weeks, begin to seek out your answers, adding information to this page as you uncover it.

> **Hope Note:** *When you have gathered the answers needed for your beginning, middle and end, block out several hours of quiet time to write your story in its entirety.*

Moving forward requires that you define a beginning, middle and end for your experience. Once you have accomplished this you can move on with a new perspective, feeling confident that you have acknowledged, and come to the most through understanding possible at this time.

> **Hope Note:** *While we don't have the power to change what has happened, we do have the power to control our reaction.*

Step Five:
Finding Forgiveness

Purpose: To release ourselves from unnecessary pain through the act of forgiveness.

"The important thing to remember when it comes to forgiving is that
    forgiveness doesn't make the other person right;
    it makes you free."
    ~ **Stormie Omartian,**
    PRAYING GOD'S WILL
        FOR YOUR LIFE

Forgiveness is one of the hardest Steps of the grieving process and one where many people, who are otherwise doing fine in their grief journey, get stuck. I know firsthand how difficult forgiveness can be since it was one of my hardest lessons in grief.

When our anger gets stuck, it doesn't let us forgive. That is why this Step comes so much later in the grieving process. We have to release our anger and our pent-up emotions before we can get to the place where forgiveness is possible.

How do we know if we need to forgive? We know because we feel a gnawing sadness inside of us, although we may not know the cause. We do the releasing exercises, but an ache still lingers. Nine times out of ten, if we have completed the other emotional exercises of grief, this ache is caused by our inability to (or choice not to) forgive.

The interesting thing about unforgiveness is that it is a lot like guilt. It is a useless emotion that mostly hurts the person who feels it. Your inability to forgive anything or any person in your world may hurt someone else a bit, but I guarantee it hurts you and your world a hundred times more.

As a visual example, think of two goal posts set 20 feet apart. A more content and peaceful life rests just after the goal posts—all you have to do is run through the 20 foot space, blindfolded and voila, you will be closer to the life you want. It will be a little tough, granted your are blindfolded—but there is a big enough area where you should be able to break through to the other side with a few attempts. Unforgiveness is like an 18 foot wall. Place that between your goal posts and now try running toward that other side. Maybe you'll get through. Most likely, you'll get some bad bruises, or maybe a broken bone, and probably give up, believing that there really isn't a space—just a brick wall. Like a wall, unforgiveness blocks our pathway.

Forgiveness Brings Freedom

With forgiveness, we face our emotions, the good and the bad. Instead of glossing over how things actually happened, we face the reality of how our cards were dealt and how we feel the hurt and anger within. When we are unforgiving, we see our own dark sides. Only through facing this darkness, can we release ourselves from its toll. An unforgiving nature is very costly in our lives. We may find ourselves attaching to other people in unhealthy ways, punishing other people or losing hope in the world and in our peers. As you can see, we are the ones that suffer most when our hearts and minds wont let us forgive.

The first step in forgiveness is to understand all the elements of the incident we are trying to forgive. Instead of letting it hang above us like a black cloud, we say exactly how we feel, openly and honestly admitting our pain. Patricia Commins, author of *Remembering Mother, Finding Myself* writes, "Understanding the traumas is the first step toward healing. Through understanding, we gain some emotional space from the traumas that haunt us."

Who and what are we forgiving exactly? We are forgiving anything and everything that needs to be forgiven.

We may be forgiving God, a person who harmed us or a person who harmed someone we love. We may be forgiving our parents, our society, our world, or ourselves. Forgiveness does not mean that we are condoning hurtful actions. It doesn't mean that we accept the sometimes evil and inhumane actions of others. Forgiveness does not mean that we forget how much we hurt. Forgiveness simply means that we acknowledge the deep pain we feel, but choose to move past that pain. We forgive those who contributed to our pain and let their actions become part of our past, too. We can dislike what someone has done to us, but we can still forgive them and allow them to be someone new, instead of freeze-framing them in that hurtful place.

Sometimes looking at this in a different perspective can be extremely helpful. Think back and recall a time when you did something hurtful to someone. Perhaps you said something "off the cuff" that hurt someone's feelings, or perhaps you did something you were ashamed about. Take a few moments to recollect the most vivid example that you can. Now think through the series of events that led up to your action. You did something hurtful and how did the other person respond? Did they eventually forgive you? What would happen if they hadn't? What would happen if the person had stayed angry at you for that action? You made a mistake, a bad decision, or didn't think before acting, and if they didn't forgive you, they would never be able to see you how you are now. Unforgiveness chains people to their painful actions. We freeze that painful time. Can you see how that person would be missing all you could offer? Or how that person could become so focused on the pain you caused, that they would miss the other good happening around them?

A classic example is the spiteful lover. You have probably met someone like this or have seen a likeness depicted in a movie. They have been "wronged" somehow in a relationship and have become adamant that the opposite sex is "not worthy of their time." Instead of realizing they had a painful experience, acknowledging it and moving on, they continually focus on their pain. Meanwhile, one-thousand perfect matches could walk right by and they would never know. They are too busy focusing on life's injustices. Many friendships end this way. There is some fight or spat between close friends or neighbors, and instead of practicing forgiveness, people practice grudge-holding. Eventually, hearts grow bitter and less trusting.

Forgiving people also serves as a huge release. When we don't forgive, we become in a sense, that person's "judge and jury." Our unforgiveness is "their sentence." However, it is not our job to be the judge and jury over anyone. It is our job to live life. Besides, the responsibility of "judge" is one that is stressful and pain-ridden. It is certainly not a role any of us need to assume ever—especially during grief.

As I rediscovered the role of faith in my own life, I found comfort in the New Testament when it came to topics of forgiveness and judgment. I was able to see that Jesus, when faced with judgment did not react harmfully, but blessed others. This act of non-judgment allowed Jesus to retain a peaceful heart. Had he chosen to judge, he would have wrapped himself in angst. Slowly, through my studying and reading, I came to accept that it was not my job to judge anyone (nor my right). Likewise, it is not my job to defend myself to anyone who tries to judge me.

At one point in my life, I was so concerned with how others saw me. I wanted to make sure everyone had the actual facts on which to base their thoughts and opinions. If someone held what I perceived to be an unfair view, I would go to great lengths to get my own "evidence" into their hands or to defend myself. I cannot tell you how exhausting this was. Liberation came when I made the decision to truly "let go." I began to focus only on blessing others—no matter what they thought of me. I quit trying to "present my case" and instead began to live my life. Everyday I set out to live the best life, and do the best work, I am capable of doing. I will let that action speak for itself.

The Freedom brought by Forgiving One Another and Ourselves

Forgiveness means to "give as before." To quote John Bradshaw from his book *The Family*, "It means that we give up resentments and release the energy that has kept us in bondage."

Think about an event where you have not forgiven someone. Write down what emotions you feel when you recall that event. Now think back to a time before that event happened. Did you feel these emotions? You probably did not. When you forgive, you give yourself the freedom to let go of the hurtful emotions and enjoy the positive that can be found. When there aren't any positives to be found, forgiveness gives us permission to let go, move forward and grow. Realize the only way to get back to the more peaceful time is through forgiveness.

> **Hope Note:** *Gather inspiration from those who have forgiven you for small and large mistakes.*

Forgiving Someone Who Has Died

I have seen countless times, where someone has had a traumatic relationship with a person who has died. Perhaps it was a mother and child, who fought incessantly and couldn't agree through the teen years. Sometimes its a husband and wife, whose last living conversation contained words of sadness or anger.

In the absence of the relationship, the living person begins to "re-write" their story, removing the negative elements and sometimes even putting the lost loved one on a pedestal.

It's okay to be angry with someone you have lost. Patricia Commins writes, "It is impossible to have a 'perfect' relationship with anyone…the truth is we all have faults that become all too apparent in close relationships."

Unfortunately, because we are human, it is inevitable that some of us will lose a loved one during a rocky point in our relationship. Our last words may be words we will forever regret or be saddened by. While we can't rewrite history or change the past, we can let go of our anger. Even if we can't resolve these conflicts directly with the person anymore, we can still resolve them within ourselves.

Hope Note: The art of forgiveness has no earthly barriers.

Letter Writing: Focus on a situation or experience you feel angry about or that you have been unable to forgive. Write a letter to the person or situation your emotions are directed toward. Write down everything that you are mad, sad or upset about. Let it all out—don't hold back. Use any words you can to describe your feelings and emotions. If you don't like to write, speak your mind into a tape recorder, holding nothing back. Feel the release that occurs inside you as you do this. Expect tears. Expect all the anger and ugliness to emerge as you purge the incident from your system. When you are done, take the letter and burn it, or the tape and crush it. Let this serve as a symbol of your forgiveness. If you become stuck in the pain again, repeat this exercise.

Letter writing can also be used to "keep in touch" with a loved one and to "keep in touch" with ourselves. Many people find solace in expressing happy and sad emotions on paper. One bereaved woman described her writing in this way:

> *"When I write to Phil, it gives me a sense of talking to him. I let him know everything that happened at work and what his friends were doing, etc. Some people think it must take an awful lot to write to him so much but in reality I think it brings me closer to him in my heart and in my mind."*

Self-Forgiveness and Self-Love

Even when we have been able to forgive those who have hurt us, we often cannot forgive ourselves. Many of us unfairly hold ourselves prisoner to unrealistic standards that we would never expect of another person.

Patricia Commins writes, "self-love is the only way to move forward. It is the only cure for the wounds of the soul, the only escape route from the negative patterns of the past. The more severe the trauma, the more urgent the need."

Writing a letter, as mentioned on the preceding exercise, can also be a very valuable tool for forgiving ourselves. The act of putting pen to paper allows us to articulate our feelings, face them, and most importantly, forgive ourselves for them.

Self-Forgiveness Reality Check Exercise: Recall an incident for which you have not forgiven yourself. Write about the incident in your journal.

Now close your eyes. Imagine a morning where you are sitting in your kitchen with a cup of coffee one morning when a dear friend knocks on your door. Your friend is trying to hold back her tears, but you know she has been crying from her tear-stained face. You invite her in and she crumbles into the chair across from you. When you ask what is wrong, she bursts into tears, mumbling her story of sadness through strained breath. Imagine that her story of sadness is the same or parallel to the event recorded in your journal.

Visualize yourself advising your friend. What do you say? Do you make her feel worse, by amplifying her mistake? Do you lecture her, implying she should hold herself hostage to her mistake and let it cause unhappiness throughout her life? Or do you take a different tactic? Take a moment to thoroughly visualize your response, then write about it in your journal.

A true friend would not let another friend suffer indefinitely—even for the worst of actions. Instead, a true friend would suggest accountability while encouraging self-forgiveness and forward movement. Try offering yourself that same wisdom.

Hope Note: Self-love and self-forgiveness come when we treat ourselves as we would a dear friend.

Try another quick visualization. This time imagine it is you who is crying at the table. Take the same attitude with which you responded to your friend, and apply it to your situation. Write out the council you receive in your journal. Try this exercise whenever you feel you are being unforgiving to yourself.

Patricia Commins knows that "As we move into a place of deeper self-love, we draw into our lives gentleness and nurturing. We cannot erase the trauma and pain of our past... we can open ourselves to the redemptive power of healing, allowing love and understanding to take the place of anger, bitterness and self-loathing. We invite love and healing into our lives, which can come at any time and any age. It does not depend on having a lover, spouse, children or even close friends. It does not require money, worldly success or fame. All we need is to look at the [person] in the mirror, acknowledge the journey she has traveled thus far and give her permission to be."

> **Hope Note:** *Through journaling, acknowledge your journey. Acknowledge your self and forgive your self. Give your self permission to "be."*

Unblocking Unforgiveness: If we have lived a life where we have not practiced forgiveness, we have likely built a wall of pain and hurt inside. Unearthing all of this unforgiveness is the first step toward healing.

In your journal or *Companion Workbook*, write down everything you can recall from your life that has gone unforgiven. Include the ways you have not forgiven others and include times when you did not forgive yourself. Let this list build throughout the upcoming month.

This list serves as your pathway to freedom. It will take time, but working through each event on your list, by using the exercises in this chapter, will grant you peace and freedom from the bondages brought by not forgiving one another or ourselves.

Simple Self-Love Exercise: For those of us who have not practiced self-love, it can be a difficult concept to grasp. Begin with a simple gesture of self-directed love. Perhaps it is five minutes of uninterrupted reading, or a hot bubble bath, or a walk in nature, or meeting a friend for a cup of coffee. It can be anything that validates the importance of treating yourself well. Create a list in your journal of simple ways you can express self-love. Affirm your value daily by practicing one of these exercises.

> ***Hope Note:*** *Learn the non-judgemental and "destressing" art of forgiveness. Also learn to forgive yourself. Not being able to forgive usually hurts us more than it hurts anyone else.*

Step Six:
Finding Faith

Purpose: To explore, rebuild and repair our faith.

"Whatever religion we choose to accept, we have to recognize that it has led others through their 'dark valley of the shadow of death' in the past, and it will do so again. We are not the first to tread that bleak path, even as we know we will not be the last."

~ **Robert J. Marx, Susan Wengerhoff Davidson,** FACING THE ULTIMATE LOSS

There is a reason that faith comes later in the grieving journey rather than earlier. Faith is a complex and difficult concept to grapple with on any given day, let alone during a time when it has been pushed to the edge. As Robert J. Marx and Susan Wengerhoff Davidson write in *Facing the Ultimate Loss: coping with the death of a child*, "All we know is that we are in pain, and quick fixes are the things we reject most quickly. In a time of suffering, we all recognize that faith is not an easy thing to grasp. There are so many moments when we are too depressed to even listen to what our faith has to offer."

It is for this very reason that faith comes later in our journey. We begin to seek out or reunite with our faith after we have faced many of the emotions of grief. That does not mean that God isn't with us while we grieve. Many people can, and do, find solace in the grace of God throughout their journey. But for many others, not only do we experience loss, but we may question the foundation of our spirituality. Suddenly we are living in a foggy world with a new question at every turn—questions that do not have easy answers.

The fact that there aren't easy answers makes the Step of restoring, or finding, or renewing faith similar to much of the grief process itself. We do not have a book filled with easy answers. Instead, we move forward, step by step, until we emerge on our own pathway, toward a new beginning of understanding.

Hope Note: Recognize that the process of restoring faith does not happen overnight. Give yourself time and space to explore and rebuild your faith.

A Fork in the Road

In my work with those who are grieving, I have noticed an interesting phenomenon. For some people, loss serves as a catalyst, increasing their faith—for others, loss becomes the reason they turn away from their faith.

I have heard stories of people who never had God in their life, turn to God for the strength to survive. Many people find comfort, knowing God is there to receive their loved one.

"It just occurred to me this past week, that if my love is able to transcend this mortal life, that his[my deceased sons] love for me is also able to do
the same." ~Janice, a Grief Steps member

Other people find that their image of God is destroyed. They question how God could let this happen and become frustrated when faith communities can't support or understand their deep hurt.

As I worked with professionals and debated why some people are drawn to God's presence while others withdrawl I found a few ideas which may resonate with your own experience.

Where is your focus? Some grievers focus on the tragedy itself, letting all the surrounding activities and gestures swirl into the oblivion of their grief. These grievers do not see, or quickly forget, the people that reached out to them, the people that sat with them late into the night to offer comfort. When we cannot see that "God is in the little things," that God is in people's gestures, we tend to stumble on our own faith.

Who is accountable? Depending on your personal belief system, you may hold God accountable for every twist and turn life takes. If this describes your faith, a separation from God is likely. After all, we must wonder how God could let this happen. As we question God, we question our own patterns of faith. Following the natural fight or flight response, we move away from our faith—a faith that has hurt, instead of helped us. However, this is when we have to explore our faith more than ever.

There is a wonderful book that I consider a must-read for those who face grief. The book is written by Rabbi Harold S. Kushner and titled *When Bad Things Happen to Good People*. While an excerpt cannot do justice to the difficult topics and questions Kushner covers, I want to share this passage:

"Insurance companies refer to earthquakes, hurricanes, and other natural disasters as 'acts of God.' I consider that a case of using God's name in vain. I don't believe that an earthquake that kills thousands of innocent victims without reason is an act of God. It is an act of nature. Nature is morally blind, without values. It churns along, following its own laws, not caring who or what gets in the way. But God is not morally blind. I could not worship Him if I thought He was. God stands for justice, for fairness, for compassion. For me, the earthquake is not an 'act of God.' The act of God is the courage of people to rebuild their lives after the earthquake and the rush of others to help them in whatever way they can.

"I don't know why one person gets sick, and another does not, but I can only assume that some natural laws which we don't understand are at work. I cannot believe that God 'sends' an illness to a specific person for a specific reason. I don't believe in a God who has a weekly quota of malignant tumors to distribute, and consults His computer to find out who deserves one the most or who could handle it best. 'What did I do to deserve this?' is an understandable outcry from a sick and suffering person, but it is really the wrong question. Being sick or healthy, [happy or sad], is not a matter of what God decides that we deserve. The better question is 'if this has happened to me, what do I do now, and who is there to help me do it?'"

The Push-Pull of Comfort: Another reason people are conflicted by faith has to do with finding their own sense of peace. For many, the very thought of finding any solace or comfort seems a betrayal to their loss. "Why should I be happy when _____ will never know another day on earth?" "Who am I to seek comfort when I have lost my job and cannot amply provide for my family?" One hand reaches for the comfort that can only be provided by faith while the other hand pushes it away.

When we find ourselves engaged in the push-pull of faith, we must continue to work with the exercises that help us to seek meaning, redefine our life, and find purpose in our loss to carry forward. When we commit to moving through this haze, our conflicting emotions become only temporary and we will be able to surpass them.

A Child's Prayer

Now I lay me down to sleep,
I pray thee Lord my soul to keep.
If I should die, before I wake,
I pray thee Lord my soul to take.

This simple prayer, usually learned in childhood, has brought comfort to many for decades, demonstrating the safety and power a person may feel when in the arms of God.

Faith Communities and Anger

It's common to question God in these dark times. We may lose our faith in God, a faith we thought would never change or waiver. This is okay. The Psalms are filled with passages where God is questioned.

"My God, my God, why have you deserted me?
...Why are you so far away?
Won't you listen to my groans and come to my rescue?
...I cry out day and night, but you don't answer,
...and I can never rest."
~Psalm 22: 1,2 (Contemporary English Version)

We have the right to feel passing anger, but it is also important to not let our anger destroy our faith.

In *The Grief Recovery Handbook*, John W. James and Russell Freidman write, "We have to be allowed to tell someone that we're angry at God and not be judged for it, or told that we're bad because of it. If not, this anger may persist forever and block spiritual growth. We've known people who never returned to their religion because they weren't allowed to express their true feelings. If this happens, the griever is cut off from one of the most powerful sources of support he or she might have." For most of us, this loss of faith is temporary and if we ask our clergy person or faith community, they will willingly help us with this struggle. It is common for grievers to yell, scream at God or lose faith. One should not feel guilty for such emotions. Like many other aspects of grief, this internal search is part of the process.

> **Hope Note:** *Are you in a faith community that can give you the support you need? If not, is there another support community available to you?*

If you find yourself in a faith community that cannot handle your anger, you must re-evaluate your needs. Your primary need is to be in a group of believers that can accept your human feelings. Seek out a support group or community that can walk with you through this dark time. If your faith is important to you, do not shut yourself off from it for fear that no one will understand or accept you. After you have moved through your journey, you may want to consider going back to the faith community where you could not find initial support and begin a support group.

Anger as Evidence of Faith

In its basic sense, our anger is an affirmation of our faith. Authors Marx and Davidson summarize this well when they write, "When we lose a child [or someone or something], we so often become the victims of our anger—anger at a husband or wife, anger at a doctor, even occasionally at the child who has been taken from us. Of all the rage we experience, none may be more bitter than our anger toward God. 'How could a loving and kind God do this to me?' Even the rage of a betrayed husband or wife could not be more bitter. After a lifetime of trust, how could that God of justice and loving-kindness allow this terrible injustice? The angry question can be seen as an affirmation and accusation. After all, the very anger we feel is based upon the fact that we believe. We cannot be angry with someone who does not exist."

Hope Note: Think about any anger you feel. How does that serve as a testament to your faith? Consider writing about your feelings.

What Do I Believe?

As we stand at our own crossroad, we must look at our life and evaluate our faith. Is our faith a part of us or is it simply something we have inherited and accepted blindly? Have we really believed prior to our loss—or have we just gone through the motions? What does faith mean to us? What do we seek to find? Once we identify our basic need and belief system, we can begin to move toward the communities and materials that will be the most helpful. Faith, by definition, should be something that encourages and supports us in our day-to-day living.

In *Transcending Loss: Understanding the Lifelong Impact of Grief and How to Make it Meaningful*, author Ashley Davis Prend offers a wonderful view on the purpose of faith and religion. "The purpose of religion is to be a vehicle, an avenue of facilitating spiritual connections with the Divine. And yet, as we've seen, many people find that religion isn't so much a helpful bridge to spirituality as a gated tollbooth with padlock and chains. In rethinking how to unlock the gate and restore free transportation, some people find that they choose to abandon their childhood religion. They choose to go on a search for a new faith community that can support rather than condemn, that can nourish rather than diminish, that can sustain rather than victimize."

Perhaps you are someone who has never had a true presence of God or faith in your life, and yet know something is missing. You are right to assume that the "missing piece" may be God-related. I have not found anyone who has overcome severe adversity or tragedy without some form of faith—however they choose to define it. If this is a new path for you, try some of the Simple Steps found later in this chapter and/or discuss faith with others. Identify people you admire and ask them for recommendations about religious and spiritual books and resources.

Hope Note: Use a few pages in your jour-nal to explore your feelings about faith and its role both past and present in your life.

No song expresses more beautifully, than Amazing Grace, how faith can play a role in both the past and the present of a person's life. Written by John Newton, this universally recognized song has offered spiritual comfort since 1829. Easily recognizable by its familiar first verse, it has brought comfort to many during times of difficulty. Most of us know the first verse, yet there is great comfort to be had in reading (or singing) the song in its entirety.

Amazing Grace

Amazing grace! How sweet the sound
That saved a wretch like me!
I once was lost, but now am found;
Was blind, but now I see.

'Twas grace that taught my heart to fear,
And grace my fears relieved;
How precious did that grace appear
The hour I first believed.

Through many dangers, toils and snares,
I have already come;
'Tis grace hath brought me safe thus far,
And grace will lead me home.

The Lord has promised good to me,
His Word my hope secures;
He will my Shield and Portion be,
As long as life endures.

Yea, when this flesh and heart shall fail,
And mortal life shall cease,
I shall possess, within the veil,
A life of joy and peace.

Simple Steps

As we search to find our path toward faith, the following anonymous poem can be comforting to recite. It offers a simple gesture of trust when we are feeling lost and our faith is being tried.

Prayer of Faith

We trust that beyond absence
There is a presence.

That beyond the pain
there can be healing.

That beyond the brokenness
there can be wholeness.

That beyond the anger
there may be peace.

That beyond the hurting
there may be forgiveness.

That beyond the silence
there may be the Word.

That beyond the Word
there may be understanding.
That through understanding
there is love.

~Author Unknown

Keeping in Touch: Micki McWade, author of *Daily Meditations for Surviving a Breakup, Separation or Divorce* writes, "Staying in touch with God on a regular basis, brings us serenity. This is true regardless of the circumstances. Some will ask 'How can God let this happen to me?' but this is a trap that only brings despair. God doesn't make things happen to us, but will comfort us and give us strength. He will provide us with the tools to go on, if we ask. He comes to us at our invitation."

Psalm 23: 1-4(KJV)

The LORD is my shepherd; I shall not want.
He maketh me to lie down in green pastures:
he leadeth me beside the still waters. He restoreth
my soul: he leadeth me in the paths
of righteousness for his name's sake. Yea, though I
walk through the valley of the shadow of death, I
will fear no evil: for thou art with me...

Hope Note: How can you make space for faith in your life?

The Act of Prayer: Praying does not require anything accept your own willingness. In a time of suffering do not be concerned about a "right" way to pray or a "wrong" way to pray. Take a walk and talk to God. Let Him know how you feel. Let Him know what you need. Think about this communication as you would any other relationship. If you were angry with someone, what would happen if you retreated into yourself instead of ever voicing your feelings? A wall would form between the two of you. When we communicate our innermost thoughts to God, like with any other relationship, we keep the walls at bay.

If you have built a wall between yourself and God, then begin to pray that the wall will crumble. Ask God how to reach and how to break the wall down. Remember that God is not forceful, He comes by invitation—He comes the moment you open your heart and ask Him to be present.

This process become especially important for anyone who is angry with God. While people may argue that our anger is misdirected, we need to forgive God in our hearts so that we may mend and move forward in our relationship with Him.

Even before I faced significant tragedy in my life, I have always loved the anonymous poem, *Footprints*. I'll share it with you as we conclude our Step through faith.

Footprints

One night a man had a dream.
He dreamed he was walking along the beach
with the Lord. Across the sky flashed scenes
from his life. For each scene, he noticed two
sets of footprints in the sand; one belonging
to him, and the other to the Lord.
When the last scene of his life flashed
before him, he looked back at the footprints in the sand. He noticed that many
times along the path of his life there was
only one set of footprints. He also noticed
that it happened at the very lowest and
saddest times in his life.
This really bothered him and he
questioned the Lord about it. "Lord,
you said that once I decided to follow you,
you would walk with me all the way. But I have
noticed that during the most troublesome
times in my life, there is only one set of footprints. I don't understand why when I
needed you most you would leave me."
The Lord replied, "My precious, precious child,
I love you, and would never leave
you. During your times of trial and suffering,
when you see only one set of footprints,
it was then that I carried you."

~ *Author Unknown*

Step Seven:
Finding Meaning

Purpose: To understand that even
the deepest tragedy can bring meaning,
and to uncover that meaning.

"To everything there is a
season, and a time for every
purpose under Heaven:
A time to be born, and a
time to die; A time to break
down and a time to build up;
A time to weep, and a time
to laugh; A time to mourn,
and a time to dance."
~Ecclesiastes 3:1-4

When we grapple with sudden loss, we are forced to reconsider some assumptions about our selves and our lives. We may feel vulnerable and that life is tenuous. We may begin to question whether or not the world is meaningful and orderly. We may see ourselves as weak and needy for the first time.

You may have thought, "[Enter your loss] can't happen to me." But it did happen and you may no longer feel the world is a safe place. Feelings of vulnerability can bring on a sense of doom.

In *Trust After Trauma*, Dr. Aphrodite Matsakis writes, "The just world philosophy cannot explain what happened to you. You used to think that if you were careful, honest, and good, you could avoid disaster. But the trauma taught you that all of your best efforts could not prevent the worst from happening. So, while you would like to believe that the world is orderly, and that good is rewarded and evil is punished, you had an experience that contradicts these beliefs."

Hope Note: *Explore in your journal how your experience has changed your perception of the world around you.*

When our foundation is swept from beneath us, we begin questioning the fundamentals of life. As crazy as it seems, this shattering of assumptions is necessary in grief. We must re-evaluate what we once held as true, move through the ruin and create a new foundation based on what we have learned. In Step Seven we begin this process through redefinition of ourselves and the world around us.

During this Step we seek to find meaning in our loss, Dr. Francine Cournos, author of *City of One,* states "So much attention is given to the feelings of pain associated with loss, but there are ways to use the pain in productive ways. It often provides the impetus to push one's abilities beyond safe and predictable limits."

How can one expect to make meaning of a suddenly ended life, an aborted relationship, the loss of a pet, a disrupted lifestyle (and the painful losses that go along with it)? These are profound questions, which are not easily addressed. There are no flip responses or boilerplate answers. However, what can be offered as a pathway to healing, are possibilities and new perspectives you may wish to investigate.

It is best to answer these questions when you have uninterrupted time. Also make sure you have cycled through many of the difficult emotions that accompany loss. Attempting to "rush" these answers will only lead to frustration. These are also wonderful questions to explore within a support group.

Hope Note: Create a comfortable space and time for completing these exercises.

Before beginning your journey to uncover meaning, there are some important points I want to cover. First, finding meaning does not happen overnight. You don't suddenly wake up one morning with some secure sense of "this all makes sense now!" Usually, meaning comes with time and reflection.

When my brother died a senseless death, I hardly believed there could ever be any meaning. Yet now, six years later, I have found myself in a place I would never have been without this experience. I have created books, web sites and tools that have walked countless grievers through their dark journey. I have received countless letters and e-mails, expressing gratitude for the support I have been able to offer.

When 9/11 occurred and people scrambled for support material, I had one of the only books in existence that dealt specifically with sudden death. However, all of this doesn't make Caleb's death any more "right" or "just." I still don't have to "like" it. But I can begin to understand that perhaps there is a meaning to everything, a structure, a form—even if it is a structure that I don't like.

> *Hope Note: Finding meaning and understanding our losses does not happen overnight. It takes commitment and time to heal.*

In Step Four: Understanding Your Story, I spoke of Logan, who had been unexpectedly let go from his high-profile job at the age of forty-eight. After devoting his life to the betterment of a company, the company let him go in a down-sizing. After Logan worked through his initial shock and anger, he began to work through the steps of redefinition and finding meaning. Logan ended up totally changing his life. He downsized his home life by putting his dream house up for sale. He bought a much smaller home, payed off as much debt as possible, and began a small cafe and bookstore with his wife. The two had grown apart over the years, yet the pursuit of this new dream brought them close in ways they never had imagined. Yet Logan could have chosen many different routes. He could have skipped these steps and chosen to wrap himself in anger and bitterness. Instead, he looked at what he knew for sure. He knew he loved to read and loved books. He knew he had always wanted his own business. He knew his relationship was at a very vulnerable point. He acknowledged his priorities and for the first time, he structured his life putting his priorities first. In the past, he had always squeezed his priorities into whatever time was leftover in his days.

> **Hope Note:** *Does this loss offer you a chance to restructure your life around the things that truly matter to you? Many times we make our priorities fit around the rest of our daily responsibilities. Can you align*

yourself more closely with your priorities by restructuring after your loss?

While finding meaning comes with time and hindsight, if we keep our eyes open we are prone to discovering many insights along our grieving path. This Step contains exercises to help you uncover new insights and foster meaning. This is definitely a Step that you will need to refer to throughout the months and years ahead as you will gain added perspective with time and reflection.

Hope Note: *Complete the exercises in this chapter that you feel comfortable with. Note your feelings about the other exercises, and try to complete them as it feels right to you.*

Learning through Loss

You may want to keep a special page in your journal (or use the designated pages in the *Companion Workbook*) to record the lessons and affirmations you learn throughout the grieving process. Any lesson, no matter how seemingly insignificant, should go on these pages. These pages serve as a reflection that we are moving forward.

This idea originally came from Patricia Ellen and was used in *I Wasn't Ready to Say Goodbye: surviving, coping and healing after the sudden death of a loved one*. Since then, I have used the exercise with many people. Pattie Ball, a member of our online Grief Steps group, offers ten affirmations of life that she learned from her grieving process:

1. "I will survive. No matter how much I hurt and I feel like I will not be able to go on, I know that I am a survivor.
2. I will take one day at a time. Each new day will offer simple reminders that my life will once again be whole, such as a bird's song or a sunny day.
3. I will write down my feelings, no matter how silly they seem at the time. As I look back at previous entries, I will be able to learn and see how far I have come.
4. I have friends and family I can lean on who will support me. I don't have to pretend that I'm not hurting for the benefit of those around me.
5. I will do something nice for someone else. That's what my father would want me to do, and by helping others, I am helping myself.
6. I will take care of myself. Exercise, doing nice things for myself, and getting rest will help me physically as well as mentally.
7. I will let others know how much their kindness has touched my heart because they may need to know as much as I need to tell them.
8. I will not lose touch with my spirituality because I am hurting. My faith is what will help me survive this pain.
9. I will not be ashamed to cry.
10. I will talk about my father and display many photos of him around my house and workspace. Locking away the memories will not make the pain go away."

Maureen Owens of Virgina, shared these lessons that she learned as a result of her grief:

1. Never take anyone or anything for granted. Life can change in a heartbeat.
2. Try to turn other's requests that seem like inconveniences at the time into moments to make golden memories. Memories and love can last forever.
3. Even though "God" seems far away, He is "there."
4. All things happen for a reason, be patient and just believe.
5. Expect the unexpected—the roller coaster and "rogue" waves of emotion. They come, but you will survive.
6. Take care of yourself in whatever way you need to, if that includes others helping you, let them know.
7. Don't expect everyone to understand what you are going through.
8. Try to find quiet time each day to pray, meditate or just "be." It helps to heal the soul.
9. Surround yourself with "light" and love.
10. Share your memories with others, they too may have memories they want to share.
11. Be kind and patient with yourself.

Hope Note: *What lessons have you learned throughout your journey? Make a page in your journal to add lessons as you discover them.*

Patricia, Pattie and Maureen chose to use the power of lessons-learned in facing their grief. This practice is both healing and empowering. Try it for yourself. It can be a great reminder of the steps you are taking and a wonderful way to become more aware of purpose and meaning. See the *Companion Workbook* for more on this exercise.

Questions for Exploring Meaning

The following questions are challenging and there is no need to answer them right away. In fact, this exercise is best a year or so down the road when you've had a bit more time to assimilate your loss. When you are ready, spend some time with these questions. Write about them in your journal. See what surfaces—and how what surfaces—might be the beginning of a new phase of life for you.

Is a change occurring? Could your loss have occurred just when a particular phase of change and growth was completed for you? Could it be that you are now being catapulted into a greater phase of growth—that in spite of your tremendous loss and disrupted life, a new you, full of vital life force and creativity is ready to emerge (or has already begun to emerge)?

What does the whole picture reveal? Look at your life in totality to this point. Think about your life prior to your loss. Then think about your life now. What lessons did you learn? What lessons can you learn?

Is there a life lesson? Every opportunity, no matter how painful, offers growth if we are strong enough to meet the challenge. What life lesson can this experience teach you? What growth might this experience encourage?

Is this a springboard to something greater? In her book *Don't Let Death Ruin Your Life,* Jill Brooke examines the link between greatness and loss. She documents many famous, high-achievers who suffered severe loss in their life or at an early age. It is fascinating to see the linkage between loss and achievement in these lives. I highly recommend examining this section of her book.

Sometimes we find meaning by being thankful. We can begin by being thankful for the littlest of things, like making it through the day. As we practice gratitude, it becomes easier and easier to increase our thankfulness. The following exercise can help you explore meaning through gratitude.

Thank You Exercise

As you continue to grow and heal you will eventually discover at least something (no matter how seemingly insignificant) for which you can express gratitude. If the expression is not available to you now, it is probably a temporary condition.

When you are ready, you might want to try this Thank You Exercise. Compared to all other acts, personal and spiritual growth is greatest through the expression of gratitude. No matter how difficult at first, expressing appreciation for some aspect of your loss (no matter how minor) can help make some meaning in the face of tragedy. Acknowledging, in writing, what was empowering and uplifting, will help you retain what was valuable and to let go of the false belief that you cannot grow or learn after your loss.

> **Hope Note:** *Every opportunity, no matter how painful, offers the opportunity for growth.*

Why pick up a pen and write a note? Why not? Just think about it. The act of writing, choosing the type of pen and paper, the color of the ink, moving the pen across the paper, seeing the words—all make what you are saying more real—more concrete. You will notice your energy shift—from confusion about what to write; anxiety at having to sort through your life for the first time (or the thousandth time); your tears as you recognize what you have lost; and ultimately, a sense of relief at having given yourself the chance to express the unsaid.

Date and save your notes in a special place or put them in your journal. Re-reading these notes after several months or years can help show how far you have come. Each time you write, you will gain new insight.

Be open to different meanings. Try one on, see how it fits. You may go through a variety of meanings as you grieve. You may think this experience happened to move you out of your comfort zone, then a month later think that this experience occurred to have you face unresolved issues. Meaning can be fluid and change over time.

I want to close this chapter with the one meaning we can all take from loss and grief. Author Micki McWade writes, "One of the 'gifts' of loss is that we have become cracked open. We are out of our normal routine and have experienced a profound shift. Our awareness has been expanded and we understand more than we did. We have more empathy for others and can relate to others on a deeper level. If we choose to reach out to others and offer ourselves and our experience, we will heal more quickly." So one gift and lesson we can take from any life loss is that of empathy and the compassion to give to others.

Hope Note: Close your eyes and take a few deep breaths. Pose the question, "What may the meaning behind this experience be?" Record the first thought that floats through your mind in your journal.

In recounting the life of Jacob, Rabbi Kushner in his book *When Bad Things Happen to Good People*, highlights a conversation near Jacob's death when Joseph came to visit him. As the two talk, Kushner shares the following thoughts of Jacob, "…he remembers that once he knew what it felt like to truly love someone. That someone, his wife Rachel, Joseph's mother, had died many years earlier, but Jacob has learned that love and memory are stronger than death, and her memory has remained with him every day since then."

Kushner goes on to say, "It seems to me that Jacob got it right. Goodness and love are two of the experiences that assure us that our lives have mattered to the world, that we have not lived in vain. Everyone who puts in an honest day's work, everyone who goes out of his or her way to help a neighbor, everyone who makes a child laugh, changes the world for the better."

Finding meaning is often a difficult step. Meaning doesn't mean that we have to change the world or rally for a cause in front of Congress. Meaning can be much simpler than that. I want to close this chapter with various meanings grievers I have worked with have discovered… perhaps you will relate to some of their stories as you embark on the quest to find your own meaning.

When my relationship ended without warning, I wondered why on earth I had been "led" to the "perfect" match, only to have circumstance break us apart. While they say "It has been better to have loved and lost..." I did not feel this. I felt angry and betrayed, like I would have rather never known how good love can be if it was only to be taken away. While my anger was intense, I continued to move forward in my life. Now, seven years later, I can see my experience more objectively. I realize that this partner entered my life at a time when I was vulnerable and insecure. He taught me courage and strength when my reserves were low. He taught me to stand up for what I believed in. These lessons gave me the strength to make some life-changing decisions in the following years—decisions I doubt I could have made without those lessons.

When I lost my dream job, I was devastated. I had spent thousands of dollars and hours of time for an education to attain a career that disappeared overnight. Two years later though, I found that job loss forced me to take a hard look at what I truly wanted for *my life. I had followed the path my parents wanted, but not the path my heart longed for. In the absence of job security, I tried new things and ended up following a creative path as a filmmaker. It is a path that has brought me more completeness and happiness than that "wonderful job" ever could.*

I went through a couple of years where I lost many close friends. Each time one of these friends would part ways I felt hurt and betrayed. What had I ever done? Why were all these people deserting me? After a series of such friendships, I had to look at the type of people I was attracting in my life. How did I end up with so many unhealthy people in my inner circle? I realized that these weren't so much "friends" but people I was trying to "save" due to unresolved emotional issues from my past. While these losses were painful, they forced me to confront my past and ultimately I gained healthier friendships and a healthier sense of self.

Step Eight:
Redefining Ourselves

Purpose: To understand the void that has been created by our loss and how that void will change our personal belief system.

"Transformation stems from a shift in perspective... it also means looking at the positives and negatives of one's life and seeing what treasures can be recovered from the rubble."
~ **Patricia Commins,**
FINDING MOTHER,
FINDING MYSELF

L oss doesn't just affect one area. The shadows of loss affect other aspects of our lives as well, requiring us to examine the emptiness that has been created. When we understand this, we can go about the business of redefining ourselves and filling the emptiness.

As you begin the Step of redefinition, understand that you don't need to know all the answers now. No one will force you or hold "a clock to your head" asking you to redefine yourself over night. Redefinition is a process. It involves soul-searching, courage and rediscovery. It takes time.

Simply stated, the question becomes, "Now what?" After expecting life to take a certain course, it has chosen it's own, far from your plans. Again, take it slow. Choose one thing that you know for certain.

Hope Note: Use a blank piece of paper to complete the exploration exercise below.

After any loss, our life tends to fall into three categories. Divide a piece of paper into three columns. Label the first column, (1) What I know for sure... or things that definitely won't change. Label your second column (2) Things that definitely will change. Label your third column (3) Things that could change—in other words, opportunities that have been created for change. For those using the *Companion*

Workbook, you'll find a sample worksheet in the Redefining Ourselves section.

Begin with column one, filling in those things that you know for sure. If you have always loved to paint, or If you love animals—record those aspects of your identity in this column. These are the stable pieces of your life.

Next, move to column three and record what has definitely changed in your life. If most of your days were spent caring for an aging parent who has now passed, you might right "full time caregiver" in column three. Perhaps you were a very active person who has experienced a physical injury or disability that will change your level of activity. Maybe you loved to travel and did so regularly, but due to a divorce or financial setback, will not be able to travel as frequently. Record any areas of your life that will undoubtedly change in column three.

Column two is the bridge between what won't change and what will change. Where have opportunities been created? Where is there uncertainty? If you were a wife or husband who has become single, there is a gray area. Will you choose to enter a new relationship? It is not important to have the answer now—just the question. Perhaps there was a hobby you shared with a best friend or romantic interest who has now left your life. The hobby may be painful to continue—but you have a choice as to whether to continue it or not. That type of option would be listed in column two.

This exercise isn't devised to make a neat life-graph that you can follow. The purpose is to have an awareness of what is left of your foundation and to identify opportunities for choice and growth. You also know where you must rebuild and where important decisions need to be made. Awareness is key. If we live life unaware, life will deal the cards for us. As you work through this exercise, you would do well to keep the Serenity Prayer nearby for easy reference...

God grant me the Serenity
to accept the things I cannot change;
Courage to change the things I can;
and Wisdom to know the difference.
~Reinhold Neibuhr

The remaining exercises within this chapter will help you uncover more of the opportunities that can be added to one of your own Shifting Worksheets. The point of this exercise is to look at life from all different angles and to become aware of what your life is—and isn't.

Hope Note: This is a future that has been "handed to us," we have not chosen it. It would be easy to fall victim to this turn of events, but by choosing actions to help with our healing, we become "emotional heroes" not victims.

Exercises for Understanding What We Have Lost

The Void: To truly acknowledge our grief, we must examine the void that has surfaced. Write about the changes you have experienced because of your loss. What areas of your life are incomplete? If you have experienced the ending of a relationship, you might have lost physical contentment in your life, closeness, love. If you have lost a parent, you may experience the void of trusted wisdom or a mentor. If you have moved, you might experience the loss of a home or community. If your job was your loss, you might be facing financial insecurity. Explore your specific void in detail. Try writing several pages about what you have lost and what the loss means to you. Likewise, loss often affects more than one area of our life. For example, if we have lost our significant other our spirituality may be affected because we question God. If it was a breakup our self-esteem and self-worth may plummet. We may not take care of ourselves physically. We may find our homes to be lonely instead of welcoming. We may stop engaging in hobbies we once enjoyed. Although the loss was in one area—our relationship area—it affects a broad spectrum within our lives.

In your journal or *Companion Workbook* explore how your loss has affected the following areas of your life:

spirituality	self-esteem	mental-health
physical health	work life	home life
hobbies	relationships.	special interests

Hope Note: When we understand the void that has been left, we can go about the business of redefining ourselves.

Another Angle: Think of your life as a house. The person that you are is the "roof" of the house. Your life experiences and the people that you know are the beams that brace the roof. What beams have crumbled because of your loss? How does that affect the roof? What beams are still there, but might be bent or crooked because your experience has challenged them? This is similar to the Void Exercise but offers another perspective. Often, when we examine experiences through different lenses, we uncover more of their truth.

Hope Note: Take a moment to analyze your loss, from the "loss' perspective." What does your loss want to tell you? How could this help you grow?

Examine Your Expectations: When we look at our expectations, we can see the depth of our loss and the hole that has been created in our life. Again, this Redefining Step helps us to understand the void so that we can then understand what is needed to fill it. Try answering the following questions about expectations:

What did you expect from this part of your life?

How do you feel life has been unjust to you?

What did you look forward to that has been taken away?

> **Hope Note:** *We need to examine our expectations and how they have been broken. Then we need to form new expectations based on our current reality.*

Exercises for Understanding What We Have Left

What Do I Love? When immersed in our sadness and feelings of loss, we sometimes forget about the wonderful things our life has held for us over the years. Try to create a list of 25 things that you love to do, or be a part of. Aim to include things that you can still engage in, despite your loss. Perhaps walking in nature, watching funny movies, baking, traveling, photography, a craft project—list as many things as possible. As you emerge from your grief, use this list to gravitate toward activities that will bring you enjoyment.

There is a slogan commonly used in A.A. groups… "Act as if…" Basically, the slogan means that we act as we wish to be, and by continually doing that we become who we want to be. Try implementing this activity by engaging in activities that have brought you joy in the past.

What My Experience Has Left Me: When we lose someone or something important to us, it is not unusual to have a sense that one was rejected or abandoned in some way. When you are feeling this searing pain and anger of abandonment, it is even more difficult to consider that your pain may be transformed into something meaningful, or that an end of a relationship (even through death) can be in any way beneficial to your growth. It can be. Especially if you were dependent on the other person for good feelings about yourself. Now is the time to look within and to affirm yourself as a person of value. It is also the time to remember and replay any positive messages you heard from your significant other before they died. Consider writing these positive messages on index cards and carrying them with you.

Hope Note: Create your own collection of positive thought cards from the guidelines provided in the "What my experience has left me" exercise.

Step Nine: Living with Our Loss

Purpose: To integrate our newly discovered meaning into our day-to-day lives and to move forward despite our loss.

"...every day, grief puts on a new face."
~Wendy Feiereisen

If we truly think about it, in its most basic sense, much of who we are is composed of the reflections of those we meet and the experiences we have gone through. Have you ever noticed that you pick up the lingo or tonal inflections of those you spend time with? Have you found yourself with mannerisms or similar interests of close friends? Perhaps, just as much as we are individuals, we are also composed of the traits and qualities we inherit from interactions with others.

In her book, *Don't Let Death Ruin Your Life*, author Jill Brooke writes, "No one that we have ever loved can totally disappear from our lives. Our loved ones live on in our gestures, our mannerisms, our beliefs and our feelings." The same can be said for any loss we have faced.

At this point in our grief journey, we have faced many of the difficult emotions that come with loss. We are at the point at which we realize life does go on—and somehow, we need to reunite with life and move forward.

When we reach this Step, many grievers become fearful that moving forward in any positive way will cause them to lose cherished memories. Guilt also shrouds us—how do we go on living happily when there is so much grief? Is that fair? Is that right?

This question becomes easier if we take ourselves out of the equation. Imagine you were talking to a close friend. He or she has suffered an incredible life loss and feels guilty to move past that loss and attempt to reunite with life. What advice would you give to him or her?

Most friends would encourage them to move forward—reminding them that the one they have lost would not want that loss to create a permanent sense of sadness or an inability to move foreword.

When we are short on courage and drained of hope, we move forward because it is the best honor and tribute we can pay to this life experience. In this Step, we explore moving forward while still honoring our loss and incorporating the lessons it has taught us.

Some grievers try to move forward without dealing with their feelings, or they try to put their loss behind them and "start over." There is a great line in the song *Name* by the GooGoo Dolls, "Scars are souvenirs that don't fade away." When we try to repress our loss, we will leave an empty place in our heart. Our goal is not to move past loss, but to incorporate this loss into our lives. One Grief Steps member offered the following analogy:

> *It's kind of like knitting a beautiful sweater, complicated, with many colors and intricate patterns and fancy stitches. The sweater is almost done. Suddenly, in a matter of seconds it unravels, laying in a tangled pile at our feet. We have a choice...we can either leave the tangled pile before us...or we can pick up the needles and knit again.*
>
> *Granted, it will be more difficult this time, because the threads are tangled. They just*

don't come off a nice neat skein anymore.
The yarn is not new and fresh. It has twists
and turns from previous knitting...even a
knot or two...and somewhere along the line,
we've also misplaced the pattern...

The person we were knitting the sweater for
is no longer here. But we keep on
knitting...Now we will wear the sweater...

How Do We Incorporate Our Loss Into Our Lives?

Make a List: Try making a list of the qualities that you valued in your loved one. Or, if you loss was not a person, list the qualities that you valued from your life experience. In the *Companion Workbook*, you'll find an exercise to guide you through this. Add to the list for a week or two until you have at least 25 qualities that were represented by your loss. Then review your list, looking for qualities that you could incorporate or improve in your own life. Write the qualities on an index card and place the card where you will see it often. You may also want to keep a journal, recording how you implement these qualities each day. Your journal may take the form of regular entries, or you can write letters to your lost loved one, sharing how you are honoring their memory. You can do a similar activity with your loved one's interests and beliefs. What did they honor? What did they believe in? What purpose did they contribute to, or hope to contribute to? How can you keep those visions moving forward?

Tell Stories that Incorporate Your Loss: As you move forward, share how this experience touched your life and what you learned. Share your funny memories. Share your sad memories. Even though you have experienced loss, you can keep fond memories alive through the stories that you share.

Create A Memory Journal: If like many a griever, you fear that you will forget precious memories, begin a memory journal. Write down your stories and memories. Add pictures or drawings if you like.

Reflections: If your loss is a person or relationship, look for the ways it has reflected into who you are. It is through these reflections we can honor our loved one, and carry their traits into the future with us. These thoughts, traits, memories and mannerisms will also serve as a link to our loved ones.

Will I Ever Get Over It?

It human nature to want to move away from, and avoid, pain. Facing our sadness and grief is complicated and often messy. We long to "rewind" to that place where we felt more complete. "How long will this go on?" ask many bereaved people. "Will this ever end?" The answer to that question rests with you. Will you complete the Grief Steps? Will you take the time to understand, process and heal? If you choose not to do the work, you sentence yourself to a difficult and turbulent road ahead. Yet, if you choose to face and process your pain, you can move beyond it.

Moving beyond our pain does not mean that it will not resurface. Deep pain and sadness, as if our loss has just occurred, can surface at odd moments and without warning. Often, when we finally feel like we are moving forward or have had a few "good months," out of "nowhere" the sadness resurfaces, the disbelief, the flashback, the rage, the insane feeling, the "whatever."

Sometimes these "grief flashbacks" occur during dates and places that trigger reminders of your experience. It might be a holiday season with an empty chair at the table. Perhaps it is an anniversary, yet there is no one to celebrate with. Maybe a movie you saw with a loved one is released onto video and the display catches your eye as you walk through the store. Maybe your lost child loved LEGOS® and when you go through the local drive-thru the "toy of the month" features those colorful square blocks. Some of these situations we can prepare for or avoid, but there will always be the unexpected "grief flashback" where the tears begin to flow and the outrage returns.

Recovery from loss is often a lifetime process. It's true that the pain lessens with time, but expect to be ambushed by grief occasionally.

In a letter Sigmund Freud wrote to a man who lost his son, he stated, "Although we know that after such a loss the acute state of mourning will subside, we also know we shall remain inconsolable and will never find a substitute. No matter what may fill the gap, even if it be filled completely, it nevertheless remains something else. And actually this is how it should be. It is the only way of perpetuating that love which we do not want to relinquish."

Know that you can find happiness again, and that happiness can be intense. It will just be different. The way grief changes is conveyed well in Wendy Feiereisen's poem entitled, "Grief."

You don't get over it
    you just get through it

you don't get by it
    because you can't get around it

it doesn't "get better"
    it just gets different

every day...
    grief puts on a new face.

In Gay Hendricks workbook, *Learning to Love Yourself,* he offers another way to look at painful events and emotions. "...think of a painful feeling as being like a bonfire in a field. At first it is hot, unapproachable. Later it may still smolder. Even later, you can walk on the ground without pain, but you know there is an essence of the fire that still remains. Take your own time, but be sure to walk over the ground again. You must do so because whatever you run away from runs you."

One of the ways we can "walk over the ground again" is to incorporate our life losses into the current day through the use of rituals.

Rituals

Rituals are an important part of life. Through rituals we are able to observe, remember and structure our beliefs and feelings. In her book, *Surviving Grief*, Dr. Catherine M. Sanders writes, "In the past, rites of passage for every shift point in life were marked by rituals, which commanded a respected place in our culture. Large extended families came together to honor the person being celebrated. During chaotic times of change and transition, these rituals provided important direction and spiritual strength."

Through rituals we create a space where we can honor and remember what we have lost. Rituals can be used to pay tribute to a life experience and also to replenish our souls. With rituals we can unite what has passed with the present day and take time to cherish this union.

Hope Note: *Life, in its most simplistic form, is a series of cycles. It is a series of "comings" and a series of "goings." We must make room for both processes in our lives.*

Some of these ideas may seem that they would bring pain, hurt or sadness, however, quite the contrary is true. They bring reality. They bring acknowledgement. They bring a place where we can truly feel our experience. When we don't do this, when we deny our pain and sadness, it burrows deep, only to erupt at some point—usually in an unhealthy way.

Life, in its most simplistic form, is a series of cycles. It is a series of "comings" and a series of "goings." We must make room for both processes in our lives. We are very good at the "comings." We celebrate with childlike hearts when a new child is born, or there is a birthday, or a marriage—if only we could learn to honor the passages of "goings" with half the tribute we give to our celebrations, life would take on more sense and meaning.

Here are some examples of how people I have known used rituals to honor their grief work:

Anniversary Candle: On the numerical anniversary of the loss (for example the fifth of every month) light a candle and take 30 minutes to reflect on what the loss has meant for you. What do you miss? What have you learned? What have you discovered?

Yearly Reprieve: On the yearly anniversary, take a day or two to go to a quiet place that you associate with your loss. Spend the time recalling memories, looking at photographs or reading letters.

Give of Yourself: On the day or dates of your choice, give to others in a way that helps you recognize your loss. For example, if your loss involved the ending of an abusive relationship, you might volunteer at a shelter.

Balloons: A member in one of my grief groups shared a story about releasing balloons. On her deceased step-daughter's would-be 20th birthday, the family gathered 20 purple balloons (her daughter's favorite color) and released them, watching them float into the sky.

Pillow Comfort: Another grief group member shared the undertaking of making a quilt and pillow. She collected soft t-shirts, fabrics and reminders of the lost loved one and sewed them into a remembrance.

Collections: Many people find starting a memory collection to be valuable. One woman I know lost a husband who loved motorcycles. Each year, she now adds a new motorcycle ornament to her Christmas tree.

Host a Get Together: You may choose to invite a group of close friends over for a quiet night of reflection and memories. Share stories and pictures. Show any home movies you might have of your loved one.

Donate: One group member donates a book to her local library each year. The book is always authored by one of her son's favorite authors.

Make A Family Tree: Begin recording your ancestry. Great strength can be found in honoring the cycles of life and discovering the courage and challenges faced by our ancestors.

Light a Candle: Select a beautifully scented candle. Throughout your difficult days, light the candle as a reminder of the passage of your life that has ended. Let the light of the candle offer you comfort. You may want to spend a certain amount of time near the candle recalling pleasant memories or writing in your journal.

> *Hope Note: I encourage each of you who read this book to choose a special votive candle and light it in honor of all of the many other readers of this book that you do not know. Say a prayer for them and their journey. As you do so, know that across the country, many people are also saying a prayer for you—including myself.*

Find Quiet: Take a minute or two at the same time each morning or each evening to visualize a favorite memory.

Our rituals need not be complex, just simple reminders to help us incorporate the significance and memory of our loss into our lives, as we move forward.

> *Hope Note: Take an evening this week and think about what rituals feel good to you. What would help you to honor and create space for your loss? Choose one ritual to begin and choose a date. Write your ritual on your calendar and follow through. Healing involves many steps—let this be one of them.*

How to Create Your Own Ritual

Creating your own ritual may seem like a difficult task, but it doesn't have to be. To begin, ask yourself what you are trying to remember or celebrate. For many, a ritual on the anniversary of the loss is valuable. Others find they'd like to create on another memorable day. If you have lost someone through death, their birthday might be a day for reflection. There are no limits on rituals. You can have one each season of the year, or one annually or every other year. Think about the purpose of your ritual as you decide on frequency. For most who are grieving, the ritual period becomes a time of breaking away from the day-to-day demands so we can experience our grief fully and focus on the memories associated with our loss.

Next, decide if you want the ritual to be just for yourself or if you want to share it with others. You may find that having a group of friends engage in the ritual is helpful. Others like this time to explore their emotions by themselves.

Where you should conduct your ritual is the next question to answer. There may be a special place that you associate with your loss. You may want to stay close to home or you may wish to travel overseas. Again, keep your purpose in mind as you choose your location.

Here are a few rituals that were included in *I Wasn't Ready to Say Goodbye*. Pamela Blair and I found these to be extremely helpful to those who completed them. Feel free to adapt these to rituals to suit your needs or to use them as a springboard for other ideas.

Karen was living in France, when her mother died suddenly at the age of 50, leaving her father alone in the United States. Each year, Karen returns home for a week over the anniversary of her mother's death. She and her father use this time to recall their memories and visit the grave site.

Jessica, Monica, Laura and Allie were close college friends, all living together. When Laura was killed suddenly in a car accident, the other three young women were torn apart. Each year, on the anniversary of the death, the three women get together and take a cruise. They recall their fun college days together. It has been five years since these women graduated and they still continue with this ritual.

Karl lost his well-paying job four years ago, only to discover that life would lead him down a new path that offered more fulfillment. Each year, he spends the day he was fired, talking to college kids about the important of choosing a career that matches your inner self and dreams.

Hope Note: Rituals are an important part of life. through rituals we are able to observe, remember and structure our beliefs and feelings.

David wanted to be alone on his deceased son's birthday. He rented a small cabin in the mountains and took nothing with him but spare clothes. He walked in the mountains, absorbed the beautiful scenery and "talked" to his son.

Tania lost a close friend due to some choices she holds herself responsible for. Each March, as the Michigan snow gives way to spring, Tania began to spend one weekend writing letters to friends, setting up lunch dates and connecting by phone. She found the ritual to be so rewarding that she now does it at the start of every season.

Cassandra, a single mother, was lost after the sudden death of her daughter. On the anniversary of her death, she asked her ex-husband to watch her other children. She took the weekend to write, cry, watch movies and look through old photographs.

Hope Note: Which of the ritual ideas sounds comforting to you? Make a few notes of what would be comforting in your time of need. Take some quiet time to sit and think about what might help you to heal. Then commit to a ritual. Mark the dates on your calendar.

A Simple Step

Our goal is not go on as we did before our loss—to do so would dishonor the experiences we have gone through. Our goal is to integrate our loss with who we are, at find new meaning and new joy. Life will not be as it was before, but life can be fulfilling, meaningful and even joyous.

If this chapter seems overwhelming and you cannot decide where to begin, start with a simple step. What is one change you can make, no matter how small to honor your loss? Can you start each day with a smile? Can you treat others in a more kindly manner? Can you listen to others more? Think of your own simple step, and then make it part of each and every day.

Step Ten:
Accepting
Our New Life

Purpose: To take responsibility that life is ours to be lived to the fullest.

"What the caterpillar calls the end of the world, the master calls a butterfly."
~ Richard Bach

One might think that after exploring all these steps, this would become the easiest chapter to write, and the easiest chapter to read. After all, we have gone through so many exercises, stages and explorations together. However, I have found this to be the most difficult chapter to write. Perhaps that is because of the power of change. Throughout this book we have dealt with understanding our crisis and assimilating our loss into our lives. At this point, we are on the cusp of emerging from the grip of grief and coming out "the other side" into new territory. Such significant change often elicits anxiety and a bit of fear. It is at this point we can be so tempted to turn back toward our grief, rather than move on. It can be easy to convince ourselves that we can't really move forward, and sentence ourselves to stay "stuck." That is the challenge we both face here... how do I give you some parting words to retain the strength that has brought you this far, and how do you hold onto that strength after you close the cover of this book?

If you haven't joined us already, this would be a perfect time to join the online support group that I monitor. In this safe and secure e-mail group, grievers share their journeys, trials and triumphs. To join, simply go to www.griefsteps.com and click on the Online Group link. We would love to support you as you move forward. As wonderful as the group is, I want to give you more as you "graduate" from this phase of grief and move forward. You have worked hard to get here. I have tried hard to help guide you. While you have learned much already, there are more lessons I would like you to carry forward.

We can only rejoin society and accept and affirm life as we are ready. We must complete all the Grief Steps to truly lead a complete life. It is not a process that we can force, but it also is not a process we should hide from. It is not a process that will happen automatically, we must take a step forward to meet life and trust life, with a willing heart. This will not happen all at once. It is like learning to walk. Our first steps are likely to be wobbly, unsteady, and we will likely fall. With a support group around us, we can get up and try again—slowly building our courage until we can walk forward and meet life with open arms.

Defining Priorities and Stepping Toward Fulfillment

If loss brings one disguised gift, it is the gift of evaluation, reflection and change. We often go about our days on autopilot, moving moment-to-moment without much thought. When loss lands in our lap, the disruption creates a pause where we are given the opportunity to reflect, re-evaluate and rebuild. One of the best ways to honor our experience is to use it as a stepping stone to be more true to our heart's desires—and to be more present in day-to-day life. We learn to turn off that autopilot and we quit letting the moments wash together. We take control of our directing our lives toward our true desires.

Uncovering those true desires and deciding what or how to change takes time, thought, reflection and healing. The following questions can help you take a look at your life priorities and focus on what truly matters to you now.

1. What are the most important elements of life for me? (Often you'll discover a common thread in your choices.)
2. Based on what I've learned, how would I describe a fulfilling life for myself?
3. What steps can I take today to move toward that fulfilling life? What steps can I take tomorrow?

"Little by little, just as the deaf, the blind, the handicapped develop with time an extra sense to balance disability, so the bereaved, the widowed, will find new strength, new vision, born of the very pain and loneliness which seem, at first, impossible to master."
~ Daphne Du Maurier,
The Rebecca Notebook

Accepting Change

After facing a significant loss, it is common to see a shift in our circle of friends. We have faced a profound experience and with that experience comes a new knowledge and new needs. We often find that we see things in a new or different light, and our needs from/and for others change with this new vision. Likewise, many friends and acquaintances will not understand the change we have gone through and wish for the "self" we once were. A member in the Grief Steps support group, wrote:

"My friends were there for me in the beginning and for that I am very grateful. They were all wonderful in those first agonizing days when my son died, but then time went on and some of them expected me to return to my old self. Well, that didn't happen. Some friends expect us to 'get better.' Often they think there is a schedule to follow but grief does not have a timeline, and we each grieve at our own pace... and that pace is usually far longer than our friends (having moved on with their lives, as well they should) have the time or patience for. Sometimes they can't relate to the 'new person' we have become, and sadly we drift apart."

When we experience loss, we make something very difficult and very sad— very real. If we honor our loss, speak of our loss, and incorporate it into our life (which is healthy, and our right to do) it means that those who are around us will be reminded that loss is very real. And can happen to anyone at any time.

Many people are ill-equipped with the emotions and strength to face that reality. That is why they want us to "get back to normal"—they want us to get back to where they don't have to look that reality in the eye. But that is a place we cannot go back to—at least not if we choose the healthy path. For this reason, we will shed many friends or notice friendships change. Although I don't know what experience Joni Mitchell was facing, the lyrics from her song, "Clouds" are very powerful:

> *And now my friends are acting strange*
> *they shake their heads,*
> *and tell me that I've changed*
> *well there's something lost*
> *and something gained*
> *in living life this way...*
>
> *I've looked at life from both sides now,*
> *from up above, from near and far*
> *and still somehow*
> *it's life's illusions I recall,*
> *I really don't know life at all.*

I remember after Caleb died, about 3-4 weeks later, my Mom was frustrated about how some of her friends were treating her—how they just "continued on" as if nothing had changed. Their world just continued to rotate, like it was any other day. They had sent their flowers, extended their condolences, and went back to the business of living. She wondered why these people "weren't there for her anymore."

As we reflected on this together, I brought up several deaths we had witnessed in the past years—deaths where we knew the person, or the surviving family, and we were fairly close. I reminder her how we sent flowers, went to the services, expressed our condolences, and then went on with our lives.

When it happens to us— we get a "ticket" to join a "club" with "new eyes" and a "new way of seeing." The world as it once was, ceases to exist. What we once considered "normal" will never be ours again, and we are forced to adapt and shapeshift to create a "new normal." Yet when we remain open, we are often led to the very people that hold the same ticket and belong to the same club. And then we can grow together. As an example, you have come to this book. There are many support options suggested throughout this book. If you choose to utilize them, they can bring you nearer to others who hold the same "ticket." And they will continue the journey with you.

An Exercise in Hope

During our darkest days, we often spend much of our time focusing on our sadness and our loss. Developing a sense of hope, no matter how small, can be a wonderful way to lift our spirits and remind us of all the reasons to move forward.

Sarah Ban Breathnach in her bestselling book, *Simple Abundance: A Daybook of Comfort and Joy*, advocates the use of a gratitude journal. She sites this as "a tool that could change the quality of your life beyond belief." We usually think of starting gratitude exercises at a hopeful point in life—such as a New Year Resolution. However, it is in our darkest hour that we need these exercises the most. This is how Sarah explains the gratitude journal...

"I have a beautiful blank book and each night before I go to bed, I write down five things that I can be grateful about that day. Some days my list will be filled with amazing things, most days just simple joys. 'Mikey got lost in a fierce storm but I found him shivering, wet but unharmed. I listened to Puccini while cleaning and remembered how much I love opera.'

Other days—rough ones—I might think that I don't have five things to be grateful for, so I'll write down my basics: my health, my husband and daughter, their health, my animals, my home, my friends and the comfortable bed that I'm about to get into, as well as the fact that the day's over. That's okay. Real life isn't always going to be perfect or go our way, but the recurring acknowledgment of what is working in our lives can help us not only survive but surmount our difficulties."

Recognizing the positives in our lives is especially important when we are engulfed in dark times. We often focus so heavily on our loss and what isn't going right, that we can't see any of the good things. For the first few months, it will be extremely difficult to find the positives, but after that initial time period, we need to begin looking again—no matter how simple these positives might be. Your list might include something as basic as "I was able to get out of bed today." What's important is that we be open to the fact that there are positives. By recognizing them, we attract more positives to our life.

> **Hope Note:** *For one week, keep your own gratitude journal recording five positive things that happen each day. At the end of the week, write what you learned from this exercise. It will likely become an activity you will want to continue!*

Calming Exercise

Stress, anxiety, sadness, depression—these emotions can leave us knotted inside. Practicing deep breathing exercises can help us to relax and unwind our wound-up-emotions. The following exercises will help calm you during trying times.

Place one hand on your abdomen. As you inhale, you want to feel the movement in your abdomen, not in your chest. Inhale for the count of ten, then exhale for the count of ten. Repeat this ten to fifteen times for deeper relaxation.

To relax your whole body, lay down in a quiet place. Breathe deeply, slowly inhaling and exhaling. Beginning with your left leg, clench your muscles as tightly as you can for the count of three. Then relax them. Do the same with the right leg, left arm and right arm. Then move up your body tightening and relaxing your pelvis, then stomach, then chest, then shoulders, then neck and lastly facial muscles. When you have completed this exercise you should feel extremely calm and peaceful. Visualize an ocean beach or other calming scene to deepen the relaxed feelings.

And so, after all is said and done, we end up here— in the final pages of this book. First, congratulate yourself for your commitment to healing. I read somewhere that over 90% of books are never read past page 20. Reading these words shows your commitment to moving forward. You have an inner strength, you are an "emotional hero," even if you don't realize it.

In Closing...

When I look back at the many things I have gained and lost in this lifetime, I realize that most of my happiness has come from enjoying life's gifts. Likewise, I see that most of my pain has come from "holding on" when it was time to "let go."

There is great power in truly realizing that you don't get to script your entire life story. There are people, circumstances and events that will always be beyond your control. However, you can always control your reaction, and the choice of whether to ultimately wilt or grow from life's experiences. Giving up control takes the knot from our stomachs, the bricks from our shoulders.

I know I won't always like the hand that I am dealt by life. I know that the losses I have experienced to date will probably be outnumbered by the unknown losses I still have ahead. Yet, getting through my losses thus far has helped me to realize my own strength. I know that *I* will never lose my sense of self.

I've learned that "letting go" means I don't always know what's best and that sometimes what I perceive to be a "disaster" is life leading me in a new direction. I've learned not to judge that which I cannot see. Life is the greatest teacher, it is up to each of us to choose to be a receptive student. In closing, I share with you a few of the many lessons from my own "Lessons I Have Learned" journal:

I have learned that I will never have all the answers—and that I do not need them to be happy.

I have learned that the greatest gift is time.

I have learned that tomorrow need not be the same as today. Each day, each hour, each minute—I choose how I feel.

I've learned that "going it alone" doesn't mean you are strong, it often means we don't know how to ask for help.

I've learned that sometimes there are no words to make "everything better," but the touch of a hand can be a bridge of hope.

I've learned that no life is inherently "good or bad," or "better or worse." To each of us our problems and dreams are significant. From this I have learned respect, appreciation—and most importantly, understanding.

I've learned that running away will always lead us back to what we are running from—and it will probably be bigger by then.

I've learned that if I choose to ignore what life is teaching me, I will undoubtedly repeat the lesson.

I've learned that laughter is magic.

I've learned that faith is our soul's food—we cannot live long without it, or live well on "just a little."

I've learned that silence is often the best teacher.

I've learned that admitting my weaknesses makes me stronger.

I've learned that "letting go" brings peace.

I've learned that unforgiveness takes up our capacity to love others. We cannot love fully with an unforgiving heart.

I've learned that life isn't fair.

I've learned that everyday may teach me something new.

I've learned to start each day with a smile and the simple prayer:

> **God grant me the Serenity**
> **to accept the things I cannot change;**
> **Courage to change the things I can;**
> **and Wisdom to know the difference.**
> **~Reinhold Neibuhr**

"To leave the world a bit better, whether by a healthy child, a garden path, or a redeemed social condition; to know even one life has breathed easier because you have lived. This is to have succeeded."
~ **Ralph Waldo Emerson**

Appendix A

How to Help
Someone Who is Grieving

As friends, relatives or others who care, there is nothing more difficult then watching those we care about endure pain—especially the pain that comes from unexpected tragedy. As a society who is untrained in how to help, we may feel confused or unsure of how to best support those we care for. The following guidelines can help you support your loved one during dark times.

Don't try to find the magic words or formula to eliminate the pain. Nothing can erase or minimize the painful tragedy your friend or loved one is facing. Your primary role at this time is simply to "be there." Don't worry about what to say or do, just be a presence that the person can lean on when needed.

Don't try to minimize or make the person feel better. When we care about someone, we hate to see them in pain. Often we'll say things like, "I know how you feel," or "perhaps, it was for the best," in order to minimize their hurt. While this can work in some instances, it never works with grief.

Help with responsibilities. Even though a life has stopped, life doesn't. One of the best ways to help is to run errands, prepare food, take care of the kids, do laundry and help with the simplest of maintenance.

Don't expect the person to reach out to you. Many people say, "call me if there is anything I can do." At this stage, the person who is grieving will be overwhelmed at the simple thought of picking up a phone. If you are close to this person, simply stop over and begin to help. People need this but don't think or have the energy to ask.

Talk through decisions. While working through the grief process many bereaved people report difficulty with decision making. Be a sounding board for your friend or loved one and help them think through decisions.

Don't be afraid to say the name of the deceased. Those who have lost someone usually speak of them often, and believe it or not, need to hear the deceased's name and stories. In fact, many grievers welcome this.

Remember that time does not heal all wounds. Your friend or loved one will change because of what has happened. Everyone grieves differently. Some will be "fine" and then experience deep grief a year later, others grieve immediately. There are no timetables, no rules—be patient.

Remind the bereaved to take care of themselves. Eating, resting and self-care are all difficult tasks when besieged by the taxing emotions of grief. You can help by keeping the house stocked with healthy foods that are already prepared or easy-to-prepare. Help with the laundry. Take over some errands so the bereaved can rest. However, do not push the bereaved to do things they may not be ready for. Many grievers say, "I wish they would just follow my lead." While it may be upsetting to see the bereaved withdrawing from people and activities—it is normal. They will rejoin as they are ready.

Avoid judging. Don't tell people how to react or handle their emotions. Simply let them know that you will help in any way possible.

Share a Meal. Invite the bereaved over regularly to share a meal or take a meal to their home since meal times can be especially lonely. Consider inviting the bereaved out on important dates like the one-month anniversary of the death, the deceased's birthday, etc.

Make a list of everything that needs to be done with the bereaved. This could include everything from bill paying to plant watering. Prioritize these by importance. Help the bereaved complete as many tasks as possible. If there are many responsibilities, find one or more additional friends to support you.

Make a personal commitment to help the one grieving get through this. After a death, many friendships change or disintegrate. People don't know how to relate to the one who is grieving, or they get tired of being around someone who is sad. Vow to see your friend or loved one through this, to be an anchor in their darkest hour.

Adapted from *I Wasn't Ready to Say Goodbye: surviving, coping and healing after the sudden death of a loved one* by Brook Noel and Pamela D. Blair, Ph.D. (Champion Press) www.championpress.com ISBN 1-891400-27-4 $14.95

Appendix B
Grief Steps® Resources

a caring community for those living with loss

Grief Steps.Com...Offering 24/7 Support

Grief Steps® is a program created by best-selling author Brook Noel, to reach out and provide support to the many people experiencing loss in their lives. She created www.griefsteps.com to offer 24/7, free internet support to anyone needing support through loss.

Joining is Free and Simple

Simply log onto www.griefsteps.com You will find support chats, support e-mail groups, a reading room, a free newsletter and other support services. Membership is free and the support is there for you—as little or as much as you need.

Online Classes Led by Brook Noel (a full class list is available at www.griefsteps.com)

Healing Exercises

In this interactive, online course, you'll complete 10 different exercises that help you move forward through grief and resolve open issues. The exercises can be completed again and again after the class to further your healing. Brook Noel will comment on work you choose to turn in and encourage you in your journey.
Class length – 6 weeks   Cost $49

Now What? Living After Loss

This class offers a solid foundation for anyone wondering how to go on after loss. You'll learn what to expect physically and emotionally and how to take your first steps toward healing.

Class length – 3 weeks   Cost $19

Rituals to Honor Your Loved One

Rituals are a wonderful way to keep the memory of your loved one with you. This class will introduce you to different types of rituals and guide you in creating one of your own.

Class length – 4 weeks   Cost $29

When Will the Pain End?
Working through Unresolved Grief

Throughout this 10 week course, you'll learn about the different stages of grief and how to recognize which of your life losses have not been grieved completely. You'll learn exercises and tactics to heal and work through unresolved grief, which are the most common causes of sadness and depression. This is the perfect class for anyone who is having difficulty moving forward after a life loss.

Class length – 10 weeks   Cost $99

The Healing Journey: Writing through Grief

In this writing-intensive class, you'll learn how to write the story of your loss and discover its meaning. You'll create a record of your cherished memories and discover how your loved one is still in your life today. When you complete this class you'll have a very special chronicle of you and your loved ones relationship.

Class length – 12 weeks   Cost $129

How to Create Your Own Support Group

In this class you will be given assignments that will lead to the creation of your own support group by the completion of the course. You'll decide what type of support group you want to start (online or in-person), create materials to help spread the word and learn how to successfully guide your support group meetings.

Class length – 8 weeks   Cost $79

Bibliography

Adrienne, Carol. The Purpose of Your Life Experiential Guide. William Morrow, 1999.

Akner, Lois F. Whitney, Catherine (contributor). *How to Survive The Loss of a Parent: A Guide for Adults.* Quill, 1994.

Albertson, Sandy. *Endings and Beginnings.* Random House, 1980.

American Association of Retired Persons Brochure, *Frequently asked Questions by the Widowed.*

American Association of Retired Persons Brochure, *On Being Alone.*

American Association of Retired Persons web site article, "Common Reactions to Loss."

Blair, Pamela and Noel, Brook. *I Wasn't Ready to Say Goodbye: Surviving, Coping and Healing After the Sudden Death of a Loved One.* Champion Press Ltd, 2001.

Bowlby, John. *Loss: Sadness and Depression.* Harpercollins, 1980,

Bozarth, Alla Renee. *A Journey Through Grief: Specific Help to Get You Through the Most Difficult Stages of Grief.* Hazelden, 1994.

Bramblett, John. *When Goodbye Is Forever: Learning to Live Again After the Loss of a Child.* Ballantine, 1997

Breathnach, Sarah Ban. *Simple Abundance: A Daybook of Comfort and Joy.* New York: Warner, 1995.

Brooke, Jill. *Don't Let Death Ruin Your Life: A Practical Guide to Reclaiming Happiness After the Death of a Loved One.* E.P. Dutton, 2001.

Childs-Gowell, Elaine. *Good Grief Rituals: Tools for Healing.* Station Hill, 1992.

Coffin, Margaret M. *Death in Early America.* Thomas Nelson, 1976.

Collins, Judy. *Singing Lessons : A Memoir of Love, Loss, Hope, and Healing.* Pocket Books, 1998.

Cournos, Francine. *City of One.* Plume, 2000.

Curry, Cathleen L. *When Your Spouse Dies: A Concise and Practical Source of Help and Advice.* Ave Maria Press, 1990.

Deits, Bob. *Life After Loss : A Personal Guide Dealing With Death, Divorce, Job Change and Relocation.* Fisher, 1992.

Du Maurier, Daphne. *The Rebecca Notebook and Other Memories.* Book Sales, 1983.

Doka, Kenneth J (editor). Kenneth, Kola J. (editor). Hospice Foundation of America. *Living With Grief After Sudden Loss : Suicide Homicide Accident Heart Attack Stroke.* Taylor and Francis, 1996.

Edelman, Hope. *Motherless Daughters: the legacy of loss.* Delta, 1995.

Ericsson, Stephanie. *Companion Through the Darkness : Inner Dialogues on Grief.* Harper Perennial Library, 1993.

Fulber, Marta. *Grief Expressed: When a Mate Dies.* Lifeword, 1997.

Fine, Carla. *No Time to Say Goodbye : Surviving the Suicide of a Loved One.* Main Street Books, 1999.

"Final Details." Brochure by The American Association of Retired Persons.

Fitzgerald, Helen. *The Mourning Handbook : The Most Comprehensive Resource Offering Practical and Compassionate Advice on Coping With All Aspects of Death and Dying.* Fireside, 1995.

Friedman, Russell and John W. James. *The Grief Recovery Handbook : The Action Program for Moving Beyond Death Divorce, and Other Losses.* Harpercollins, 1998.

Freud, Sigmund. From a letter to Ludwig Binswanger who had lost a son.

"Forgotten Mourners." The Journal News, July 29, 1999.

Fumia, Molly. *Safe Passage : Words to Help the Grieving Hold Fast and Let Go.* Conaris Press, 1992.

Gibran, Kahlil. *The Prophet.* Random House.

Ginsburg, Genevieve Davis. *Widow to Widow: thoughtful practical ideas for rebuilding your life.* Fisher Books, 1995.

Grey, John. Gootman, Marilyn E. *When a Friend Dies: A Book for Teens About Grieving and Healing.* Free Spirit, 1994.

Gordeeva, Ekaterina. Switft, E.M. (contributor). *My Sergei: A Love Story.* Warner, 1997.

Grollman, Earl A. *Living When A Loved One Has Died*. Beacon Press, 1995.

Golden, Tom LCSW. "A Family Ritual for the Year Anniversary." Tom Golden Grief Column.

Goldman, Linda. *Breaking the Silence: A guide to help children with complicated grief.* Western Psychological Services.

Gootman, Marilyn. *When a Friend Dies: a book for teens about grieving and healing.* Free Spirit Publishing, 1994.

Goulston, Mark MD and Philip Goldberg. *Get Out of Your Own Way.* Perigee, 1996.

Halifax, Joan. *The Fruitful Darkness: Reconnecting With the Body of the Earth.* Harper San Francisco, 1994.

Harris, Maxine. *The Loss That is Forever: The Lifelong Impact of the Early Death of a Mother to Father.* Plume, 1996.

Hays, Edward M. *Prayers for a Planetary Pilgrim: A Personal Manual for Prayer and Ritual.* Forest of Peace Books, 1998.

Heegaard, Marge Eaton. *Coping with Death and Grief.* Lerner Publications, 1990.

Henricks, Gay. *The Learning to Love Yourself Workbook.* Prentice Hall, 1992.

Johnson, Elizabeth A. *As Someone Dies: A Handbook for the Living.* Hay House, 1995.

Kennedy, Alexandra. *Losing a Parent: Passage to a New Way of Living.* Harper San Francisco, 1991.

Kolf, June Cezra. *How Can I Help? : How to Support Someone Who Is Grieving.* Fisher Books, 1999.

Kubler-Ross, M.D., Elisabeth. *On Children and Death: How children and their parents can and do cope with death.* Simon and Schuster, 1997.

Kushner, Harold S. *When Bad Things Happen to Good People.* Avon, 1994.

L'Engle, Madeleine. *Sold into Egypt : Joseph' s Journey into Human Being.* Harold Shaw, 1989.

Lerner, Harriet. *The Dance of Anger : A Woman's Guide to Changing the Patterns of Intimate Relationships.* HarperCollins, 1997.

Livingston M.D, Gordon. *Only Spring: On Mourning the Death of My Son*. Marlowe & Company, 1999.

Marshall, Fiona. *Losing A Parent: A Personal Guide to Coping With That Special Grief That Comes With Losing a Parent*. Fisher Books, 1993.

Matsakis, Aphrodite. *Trust After Trauma : A Guide to Relationships for Survivors and Those Who Love Them*. New Harbinger Publications, 1998.

Matsakis, Aphrodite. *I Can't Get Over It: A handbook for trauma survivors*. New Harbinger Publications, 1996.

Mabe, Juliet. *Words to Comfort, Words to Heal: Poems and Meditations for Those Who Grieve*.

Marx, Richard. Wengerhoff Davidson, Susan. *Facing the Ultimate Loss: Confronting the Death of a Child*. Champion Press, Ltd. 2003.

McWade, Micki. *Daily Meditations for Surviving a Breakup, Separation or Divorce*. Champion Press Ltd, 2002. *Getting Up, Getting Over, Getting On: A 12 Step Guide to Divorce Recovery*. Champion Press, Ltd., 2000.

Mechner, Vicki. *Healing Journeys*. The Power of Rubenfield Synergy. Omniquest, 1998.

Melrose, Andrea LaSonder (editor). *Nine Visions: a book of fantasies*. Seabury Press, 1983.

Miller Ph.D., Jack. *Healing our Losses: A Journal for Working Through your Grief*. Resource Publications.

Mitchard, Jacquelyn. *The Deep End of the Ocean*. Penguin, 1999.

Noel, Brook with Art Klein. *The Single Parent Resource*. Champion Press, 1998.

Nouwen, Henri J. *Reaching Out : The Three Movements of the Spiritual Life*. Image Books, 1986.

Overbeck, Buz and Joanie Overbeck. "Where Life Surrounds Death." Adapted from Helping Children Cope with Loss.

O'Neil, Anne-Marie; Schneider, Karen S. and Alex Tresnowski. "Starting Over." *People* magazine, October 4, 1999. p 125.

Prend, Ashley Davis. *Transcending Loss: Understanding the Lifelong Impact of Grief and How to Make It Meaningful*. Berkely, 1997.

Rando, Therese A. *Treatment of Complicated Mourning*. Research Press, 1993.

Rando Ph.D, Therese A. *How to Go on Living When Someone You Love Dies.* Bantam, 1991.

Rilke, Rainer Maria. *Letters to a Young Poet.* WW Norton, 1994.

Rosof, Barbara D. *The Worst Loss: How Families Heal from the Death of a Child.* Henry Holt, 1995.

Sachs, Judith with Lendon H. Smith. *Nature's Prozac : Natural Therapies and Techniques to Rid Yourself of Anxiety, Depression, Panic Attacks & Stress.* Prentice Hall, 1998.

Sanders, Dr. Catherine M. *Surviving Grief.* John Wiley, 1992.

Schiff, Harriet Sarnoff. *The Bereaved Parent.* Viking, 1978.

Shaw, Eva. *What to Do When A Loved One Dies: A Practical and Compassionate Guide to Dealing With Death on Life's Terms.* Dickens Press, 1994.

Sheehy, Gail. *Passages.* Bantam, 1984.

Staudacher, Carol. A *Time to Grieve : Meditations for Healing After the Death of a Loved One.* Harper San Francisco, 1994.

Staudacher, Carol. *Beyond Grief : A Guide for Recovering from the Death of a Loved One.* New Harbinger Publications, 1987.

Stearn, Ellen Sue. *Living With Loss : Meditations for Grieving Widows (Days of Healing, Days of Change).* Bantam, 1995.

Stoltz PhD, Paul G. *Adversity Quotient : Turning Obstacles into Opportunities.* John Wiley & Sons, 1999.

Tatelbaum, Judy. *The Courage to Grieve.* HarperCollins, 1984.

Temes, Dr. Roberta. *Living With an Empty Chair : A Guide Through Grief.* New Horizon, 1992.

Viorst, Judith. *Necessary Losses : The Loves, Illusions, Dependencies, and Impossible Expectations That All of Us Have to Give Up in Order to Grow.* Fireside, 1998.

Westberg, Granger E. *Good Grief.* Fortress Press, 1971.

Zarda, Dan and Marcia Woodaard. *Forever Remembered.* Compendium, 1997.

Zunin M.D., Leornard M. and Hilary Stanton Zunin. *The Art of Condolence.* Harper Perennial Library, 1992.

Other Books to Help You Heal.... www.griefsteps.com

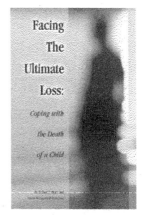

I Wasn't Ready to Say Goodbye: surviving, coping and healing after the sudden death of a loved one by Brook Noel and Pamela D. Blair, Ph.D.
ISBN 1-891400-27-4

Facing the Ultimate Loss: Confronting the Death of a Child by Robert J. Marx and Susan Wengerhoff Davidson.

ISBN 1-891400-93-2

Surviving Birthdays, Holidays and Anniversaries: a guide to grieving during special occasions by Brook Noel
ISBN 1-891400-03-7

Finding Peace: Exercises to Help Heal the Pain of Loss by Brook Noel
ISBN 1-891400-78-9